Facing Auschwitz

Facing Auschwitz

◆

A Christian Imperative

Arlen L. Fowler

iUniverse, Inc.

New York Lincoln Shanghai

Facing Auschwitz
A Christian Imperative

All Rights Reserved © 2003 by Arlen L. Fowler

iUniverse, Inc.

For information address:
iUniverse, Inc.
2021 Pine Lake Road, Suite 100
Lincoln, NE 68512
www.iuniverse.com

ISBN: 0-595-28145-1

Printed in the United States of America

Dedicated to all the victims of the Holocaust

And to

My Wife
Mary Jane
My best friend, lover, and companion
For over Fifty-Three Years.

Contents

Acknowledgements

Many individuals and institutions have been of great assistance to me in my research and writing of this book. It is impossible to name everyone and I fear I will leave someone out. Nevertheless, I will attempt to express my gratitude to as many as I can for their help in making this book a reality.

I must begin by thanking my Bishop, The Right Reverend Robert Moody of the Diocese of Oklahoma, for encouraging the priests in our diocese to take sabbaticals. Secondly, I appreciate The Society of James Mills Fellows of the Diocese of Oklahoma for their support of clergy sabbaticals, and I will always be profoundly grateful to the Vestry and congregation of St. Philip's Episcopal Church in Ardmore, Oklahoma for granting me the sabbatical that has resulted in this book.

I am also indebted to Dr. Thomas W. Gillespie, President of Princeton Theological Seminary for permitting me to live on campus during the summer of my primary research, as well as to the staff of the Speer Library at the Seminary, for their invaluable assistance. I would be remiss if I did not thank John Prager, who at that time was in the Alumni/ae Relations Office, and became both friend and guide for me during my stay on campus.

My appreciation also goes to The Very Reverend Durstan McDonald, former Dean of The Episcopal Theological Seminary of the Southwest, and to The Reverend Charles J. Cook, Professor of Pastoral Theology, for their Visiting Fellow program. I was fortunate to be a Visiting Fellow, and they provided comfortable quarters and the academic atmosphere to permit me to accomplish a significant portion of my writing.

Through many revisions, I appreciate The Reverend Charles Woltz, Canon to the Ordinary in the Diocese of Oklahoma, for his continual encouragement. I am especially grateful to the Boundary Study Group, William Rahhal, Basil Bigbie, Dr. David Rose, and Ken Beeler. Their serious reading and critique of the manuscript was very important to the completion of the book. The Reverend Dr. Thom Balmer and his wife Denise were also very helpful.

A special place in my gratitude is held for The Reverend Michael Athey, Episcopal Chaplain at the University of Oklahoma, whose Christian Leadership Series made up of a wonderful group of students, faculty, and others, read and critiqued my manuscript over a period of six weeks. Their insightful recommendations were very meaningful to me in my final revision.

I am extremely grateful for the careful copy editing of the manuscript by Jane Knight. Her expertise was crucial to the clarity of the final copy. Keith and Darci Forrester's technical assistance was invaluable to me in the final stages of the manuscript.

Finally and most important, I must express my undying gratitude to my dear wife Mary Jane Fowler, who for over fifty years has put up with me. Without her support and encouragement this book would not have existed. She has endured my constant reading and research and frequent disappearances into our study for hours at a time. She has always been there for me.

Arlen L Fowler
Ardmore, OK
June 2003

Preface

A large number of theologians in the United States and around the world have said that the Holocaust is the most important theological event of the twentieth century. The intent of this book is to allow the reader to discover some of theological questions raised by the Holocaust. Most of the American Churches have not delved deeply enough into these questions. The old answers and understandings in many areas of faith held by both Christians and Jews no longer make sense in the aftermath of the Holocaust. Perhaps it is fear or an unwillingness to change that makes so many clergy, laity, and churches reluctant to approach these issues.

This book is designed for laity to use as a study book, as individuals, in church education classes, or in some other group setting. It is purposely not a book of great length. Small, meaty, readable books are the usual favorites for study groups. Questions at the end of each chapter will help get the discussion started.

The author does not seek to belittle or destroy any person's faith, but only to pose the questions that have confronted and haunted many dedicated scholars, theologians, and Holocaust survivors. Where was God during the Holocaust? Why was God silent? Are prayers an act of futility? Does God really exist? This is not an academic exercise, rather a sincere attempt to probe the depths of our faith and provide some new perspectives. An overwhelming majority of both individuals and groups who read my manuscript agree that the time has come to rethink some of the basic tenets of Christianity, and see our faith in new way.

Prologue:
A Journey to Auschwitz and Beyond

I was twelve years old when my father invited me to go with him to a lecture at a local church. It was a special event and the public was invited. World War II had not begun, and the topic of the lecture was about the conditions in Germany under Adolf Hitler. The speaker that evening illustrated his speech with slides of scenes he had observed and photographed in Germany. I can still vividly recall those pictures of the persecution and harassment being leveled against the Jews.

I do not remember much about the content of the talk, but I will never forget the pictures. In my adolescent mind, I could not believe that a country could be so ruthless and open about its hatred and treatment of a specific ethnic group. Obviously, I was ignoring the racism toward Afro-Americans in my own community in Oklahoma.

I am telling this story because it marked the beginning of my lifelong interest in what was going on in Germany and my drive to understand why the Jews were being singled out for persecution. That curiosity remained in the back of my mind for the next few years. When the war neared its conclusion, information about the Holocaust was beginning to be made public and I was horrified.

My early curiosity never left with me until several years ago when I took a sabbatical from my parish and went to Princeton Seminary for a full time study of the Shoah. *(Sho'ah a Hebrew word for "catastrophe"and is also used to mean "the Holocaust".)* In the midst of my study, I came face to face with the silence of the Christian churches in Germany, both Protestant and Roman Catholic, during the Shoah. At that point, I shifted my inquiry to a theological investigation of the Holocaust.

I immediately discovered challenging and thoughtful books and articles by Christian and Jewish scholars wrestling with the theological implications of the Holocaust upon their faith. The questions raised by the Shoah about God, God's silence, God's absence, and God's existence were not posed as subjects for academic debate, but were about whether it was possible to piece human life and meaning back together again under the umbrella of faith.

Indeed, I was deeply troubled by the stories of the cruelty, torture, dehumanization, beatings, gassings, medical experiments, and countless other unspeakable atrocities perpetrated on millions of innocent men, women, and children. As I read about all these things, and tried to understand why they happened, the foundations of my faith gradually began to crumble. Like the many victims and survivors of the Holocaust, my understanding of God went up with the fire and smoke in the chimneys of the crematoriums.

It became painfully obvious to me that the God of my history was no longer operative in the framework of my theology, and this evolving revelation left me with a deep spiritual despair. The treasured concepts, beliefs, and doctrines of my faith lay scattered in my heart and mind like debris from a house hit by a tornado. I was ready to give up my ministry in the church. One afternoon, my wife and I sat down and talked about my disillusionment. She reminded me that most of the theologians, both Christian and Jewish, who had described the demise of the historic God, were still Christian and Jewish and they had not bailed out of their faith. She encouraged me to continue on the journey and seek a way over my spiritual abyss.

At that moment, my sabbatical took a dramatic turn, and I returned to my research and reading with an intensity and excitement I had never experienced before. Many questions still needed to be pursued, but to my surprise and joy, the more I pushed the boundaries, and the deeper I questioned, the more my inner spirit was stimulated. I still encountered doubts, even guilt, for asking the tough questions. My larger doubts and strong desire for spiritual truth and integrity propelled me to continue.

A few years later reading professor Darrell J. Fasching's book, *Narrative Theology After Auschwitz*, I felt a sense of affirmation from what he wrote. Fasching said that as a student he had a hard time understanding Paul Tillich's point that the questions were more important than the answers, but he has come to realize that Tillich was right. *(Professor Paul Tillich was one Christianity's great philosophical theologians. He emigrated to the United States in 1933 to escape the Nazis oppression of academia.)*

"I have found a fullness in the doubts and questions of my life that I once thought could only be found in answers. After Auschwitz I distrust all final answers—all final solutions. Mercifully, doubts and questions have come to be so fulfilling that I find myself suspicious of answers, not because they are necessarily false or irrelevant, but because even when relevant and true, they are, and can only be, partial. It is doubt and questioning that always lure me on to broader horizons and deeper insights through an openness to the infinite that leaves me contentedly discontent."[1]

I also found affirmation from the words of Elie Wiesel: *(An internationally acclaimed author who has written novels about the Holocaust. He is a survivor of four concentration camps and the winner of the 1986 Nobel Peace Prize.)*

"...As a general rule, I feel close to the one who asks the questions, and surely closer than to the one who insists on giving answers.

For the believer, no question can cause such anguish, such anxiety, and—why not say it?—such despair. God and Birkenau *(a death camp located in the Auschwitz complex)* do not go together. How can you reconcile the Creator with the destruction by fire of one million Jewish children? I have read the answers, the hypotheses. I have reread the theological solutions offered. The question remains question. As for answers, there are none, there ought to be none."

Wiesel then tells a story that comes from *The Black Book*, an anthology by Ilya Ehrenburg and Vassily Grossman, concerning the destruction of Russian Jews when the German armies were holding a large portion of Russia. The story is about a Ukrainian woman who is forced to watch the decapitation of her two children. "Seized by madness, she grasps the two mutilated corpses and begins to dance; she dances and dances while the killers watch her and laugh. Finally, they kill her.

The woman dancing with her dead children keeps me from sleeping. I tell myself that she is trying to communicate something to us by her dance, and from beyond her madness, and I ask myself what could that be. And, strange, I know this is linked to the conflicts haunting me concerning faith, language, the humanity of mankind, and the compassion of heaven."[2]

Both Fasching and Wiesel are right. Unless we keep on questioning, we will descend into intellectual inertia and spirit numbing dogmatism. Intellectual and spiritual boundaries are to be explored, not ignored. The fear of losing our understanding and comfort of the traditional expressions of faith, keep us chained to the past. The boundaries remain the forbidden fruit in the eyes and hearts of too many believers. Ironically, it is at the boundaries that we most often glimpse some insight into God.

In the pages to follow, I invite you to journey to with me the barbed wire of Auschwitz, and then beyond to the boundaries. It is a pilgrimage that will challenge *your* understanding of God, prayer, and faith. It is not the purpose of the pilgrimage to destroy your faith, but to expand your thinking and open your heart and spirit to a new understanding of God and our responsibilities as human beings, especially when we call ourselves Christian. As you proceed on the journey you will discover why many theologians call the Holocaust the greatest God event of the twentieth century. We cannot remain true to God if we continue to live with our minds, hearts, and backs turned away from Auschwitz. If Christianity is to salvage its spiritual integrity, it is time for us to face Auschwitz.

1

A Sound of Sheer Silence

○ ○

"Now there was a great wind, so strong that it was splitting mountains and breaking rocks in pieces before the Lord, but the Lord was not in the wind; and after the wind an earthquake; but the Lord was not in the earthquake; and after the earthquake a fire, but the Lord was not in the fire; and after the fire a sound of sheer silence."

—I Kings 19: 11b-12 (NRSV)

In March of 1945, the American Army crossed the Rhine and advanced into the heart of Germany. What the Allied armies discovered as they pushed deeper into the Third Reich would change the way the world would view humanity and civilization for generations to come.

On Wednesday, April 4, 1945, advanced elements of the Fourth Armored Division smashed through the barbed wire fences that surrounded the Ohrdruf Nord, and liberated the first concentration camp. It was the first camp to be uncovered by the Americans and it became a telling event.

Professor Bernard Weintstein writes, "…because of its unique stature it serves as a paradigm of encounter, a crossing, for Americans in particular, on the borderline between battlefield warfare, which, however brutal, yielded assumptions of military codes and conventions, and, on the other side, this landscape of limitless atrocity. Although revelations from Buchenwald and Dachau would soon dwarf those from Ohrdruf in magnitude, Ohrdruf was, nevertheless, a severing for many from what was their last innocence.

What the liberators saw (and smelled) as they entered Ohrdruf on April 4th and afterwards is recorded in their own oral testimony. They saw piles of prisoners recently shot and, in some instances, still freshly bleeding; they saw charred bodies which had not been fully cremated,...they saw remnants of living inmates, near death themselves, with emaciated limbs, skeletal crania, and bulging, haunted eyes. It was sights such as these that would cause General Eisenhower to blanch and General Patton to sicken on their tour of the camp twelve days later."[3]

As they entered each concentration camp, American and Allied soldiers stared in disbelief at the unspeakable horror of the hundreds and thousands of dead bodies stacked in neat piles or strewn across the compounds. They asked themselves what kind of human beings could do such things to other human beings? Gazing into the filthy barracks, the gas chambers, the crematoriums, the torture rooms, and the execution pits, and they wondered, how could a nation that was supposedly ninety percent Christian could be responsible for such unspeakable atrocities of such an inconceivable magnitude? Why would God allow such a horrendous thing to happen?

The same questions resonated in the minds of Jewish and Christian theologians, in the decades following the liberation of the death camps. Those theologians who studied the Holocaust, the majority agreed that it was the most important and disturbing theological event of the twentieth century. Our traditional concepts and pious views of God were found wanting and in need of serious revision. Something more than the human capacity to inflict pitiless cruelty on other human beings was revealed in the death camps like Auschwitz. *(Auschwitz is an appropriate synonym for the Holocaust and is used in that sense in the context of this book.)* Unfortunately, most American churches have not or refuse to recognize any serious theological implications in the existence of the concentration camps. There was, however, a perplexing and disturbing theological "silence" coming from the Nazi death camps, such as Auschwitz. God was in the sound of sheer silence *(I Kings 19: 11-12)* at Auschwitz, and that silence shook the foundations of the world we thought we knew. Most American churches have yet to recognize or understand the serious theological implications of Auschwitz, and appear to have interpreted the Holocaust as a tragic historical event, not as a theological event.

By contrast, the nuclear explosion at Hiroshima did catch the churches attention and we experienced all its repercussions. The shock waves from the Atomic bomb set in motion an anxious international concern over the future of the planet earth. International conferences, peace conferences, diplomatic negotiations, retaliatory policies, civilian survival training, anti-war rallies and non-proliferation treaties filled the months and years following the holocaust at Hiroshima. Many peace groups came into existence in many churches and denominations in response to the nuclear threat. Still little has been said or done by the churches concerning God's silence at Auschwitz.

Churches worldwide have conceded that the Holocaust was a barbaric thing and should never be allowed to happen again. Many memorials have been built to remember and honor the victims, and hundreds of books have been written to expose the horrors and inhumanities of the Nazis concentration camps. A number of international conferences have dedicated themselves to the study of the Holocaust.

Having acknowledged the brutality of Auschwitz and agreeing that we must never permit such a barbaric thing to ever happen again, we in our churches have gone back to business as usual. Although Jewish and Christian theologians have cried out like voices in the wilderness, telling us that something more than a horrendous pogrom took place there, the sound of the sheer silence of God at Auschwitz remains unrecognized or ignored. Our centuries old understanding of God in both Christianity and Judaism can never be the same because of the Holocaust. It has been more than half a century since the last death camps were liberated, and the American churches have yet to comprehend the full theological impact of Auschwitz.

God's silence at Auschwitz is not unlike the sound of sheer silence experienced by Elijah at Mount Horeb. In both instances, God calls the people of God to a new way of thinking and acting. For those who with ears to hear, the shattering sound of God's silence at Auschwitz presented to both Jewish and Christian theologians a set of questions that threaten long held cherished beliefs.

For Jewish theologians, the Holocaust and its "final solution" has become a question of theodicy, (*defending the justice and mercy of God especially in allowing natural and moral evil*). If Israel and its people is God's chosen ones, how could such an event take place without God's intervention or indifference? Is faith and trust in God possible for Jews after the Holocaust? For Christian theologians, because of Christian culpability in the Holocaust, how can Christians honestly say that all their doctrines are true or redemptive? What do the death camps ask about Jesus as the Messiah? These are just a few of the difficult God questions hanging over Auschwitz that churches must begin to face. Such questions are sure to disquiet our beliefs and to bring serious implications to our faith and to the Church.

Many respected scholars have considered the questions raised by God's silence at Auschwitz for a number of decades. *The Annual Scholars Conference On The Holocaust and The Churches,* founded by Dr. Franklin H. Littell and Dr. Hubert G. Locke in 1970, still meets annually to deal with these questions and many others. Decades of excellent scholarship have resulted in a great deal of serious theological reflection on the part of Christian and Jewish scholars from all over the world. Many excellent scholarly books have found their roots in these conferences.

Regrettably these tough questions have not filtered down to the vast majority of the laity in the American churches. Unfortunately, numerous clergy do not even seem to be aware of or appear to be willing to deal with the theological issues Auschwitz places before us.

If the leadership of our churches remains oblivious to the tough questions posed by Auschwitz, is it any wonder that the laity appear to be unaware of how God's silence behind the barbed wire fences has changed our understanding of God. If our adult laity is not informed about the theological questions surrounding the Holocaust, it should not be a surprise to us that our youth are even less aware. Some surveys have revealed that a significant number of students enrolling in college continue to profess ignorance about the Holocaust. Even more disturbing is that there are some students who do not believe anything like the Holocaust ever happened.

The students are but a reflection of an even greater malaise in our general population. Revisionists (*those who believe the Holocaust never happened and is nothing more than a Jewish propaganda hoax*) are still a small minority, but they represent a growing social cancer on our religious and moral attitudes. The soil for planting their deceitful ideas is found in the latent anti-Semitism in American culture, where an anti-Semitic attitude is fostered, both knowingly and unknowingly, by many individual Christians and churches.

Those Christians who read their Bible literally, will undoubtedly resent the assertion that Christianity's contribution to anti-Semitism and the death camps was a significant factor in the horrors of the Holocaust. If, however, we as Christians are brave enough to journey to the barbed wire of Auschwitz and peer into its moral chaos with an open mind, a courageous spirit, a compassionate heart, and a commitment to justice and mercy, we will be a changed people. Ironically, the movie, *Schindler's List,* did more to raise our national awareness of the Holocaust than either the churches or the scholars.

Because the Holocaust is so devastating in its dimensions, it is hard for an individual to comprehend its cruelty, brutality, and enormity. It is imperative that Christians go to the edge of that moral abyss and stare into a human version of hell. We must be still and listen and try to hear the sound of the sheer silence of God that covers Auschwitz. As we focus in through the barbed wire we have to ask ourselves how a nation that produced a Bach, a Beethoven, and a Brahms could support a political system so devoid of humanity or compassion. How could civilized human beings, the majority of whom called themselves Christian, actually plan, experiment, and create processes for the mass extermination of other human beings? What could motivate ordinary thinking, feeling, caring humans to eagerly produce and participate in an efficient system designed for the express purpose of killing millions of other thinking, feeling, caring men, women, and children?

In the end, twelve million human beings, all with hopes, dreams, families, friends, and a love of life like our own, were systematically murdered by the Nazis. Six million of that number were Jews and one million five hundred thousand were children under the age of fifteen. As we look through the barbed wire, we must remember that these men, women, and children were not killed in the crossfire of opposing armies or by bombs or artillery. Each individual was either beaten to death, starved to death, worked to death, shot to death, burned to death, tortured to death, or hanged, or gassed in the gas chambers. The number of Jews that were murdered in this bureaucratically efficient manner equals the approximate populations of the states of Kansas, Nebraska, and Oklahoma. Try to imagine the cities of Wichita, Topeka, Kansas City, Omaha, Lincoln, Tulsa, and Oklahoma City, all vacant and silent without a hint of human life. Imagine that every school, church, and synagogue; every office building, playground, college; every apartment complex, home, and shopping mall; and every factory, business, highway, and farms are all silent and empty, and you will have a vision of a human catastrophe that defies the imagination. A small glimmer of the horror of the Holocaust will begin to come into sight.

Is it possible that ordinary human beings could put on a uniform and unflinchingly become active participants in the shooting, starving, beating, torturing, and gassing to death of millions of other human beings?[4] Is it possible for a civilized nation to mobilize enough hate and fear to dehumanize an entire segment of humankind? Could human beings become so callous as to set quotas for the number of men, women, and children to be exterminated in a given week or month? When we realize that the answer to each of these questions is *yes* and that the Nazis did it, we are truly staring into the abyss of moral chaos.

To comprehend the stark reality of the answers to these questions is to enter into a nightmare of the unspeakable. The sheer mathematics of death in this human version of hell pushes our understanding of civilization over the edge. Millions of ordinary people were slaughtered for no reason other than that they were Jewish or were deemed unfit to live in the Third Reich. Using a virulent determination to accomplish the "final solution" to the "Jewish problem," and assisted by an efficient bureaucratic organization, the Nazis exterminated ninety percent of all East European Jews. The six million Jews killed in the Holocaust represented thirty percent of *all* Jews in 1939. Included among the dead were over eighty percent of the Jewish scholars, rabbis, full time students, and teachers of the Torah who were alive at that time. Evidence today suggests over a million and a half men, women, and children were sent to the Auschwitz concentration camp. When the war was over, only 60,000 survivors of Auschwitz were found. This grim statistic means that approximately ninety-six percent of all the Jews transported to Auschwitz were methodically murdered by the Nazis.

The Germans had at their disposal the latest technology, communications, and transportation to coordinate an assembly line of death. It required the cooperation of all levels of the German government and society to make the "final solution" work. Never before in history has murder been planned on such a large-scale production line process.

As we stare into this ghastly moral abyss from our vantage point decades later, we must remember one fact. From the beginning of the Third Reich, Jews were singled out for persecution and eventual extermination. The Nazis' persecution meant all Jews, whether they were half Jews, quarter Jews, or those with any amount of Jewish blood in their veins, were marked for extermination. It made no difference if they were practicing Jews or not. This "ethnic cleansing" policy of Hitler's Third Reich meant that all of Germany's Jewish families, many of whom had long and patriotic histories, were now *personae non gratae* in their own homeland. The yellow Star of David, that all Jews were required to wear pinned to their clothes, was destined to be a one way ticket to a death camp and a gas chamber that had been designed by some of Germany's best architects and engineers.

A serious look at Auschwitz will immediately raise troubling questions about humankind and about God. We cannot stare through the barbed wire of Auschwitz and come away with our previous optimistic views of humanity, civilization, or God. Indeed, to look at the pillars of fire and the clouds of smoke from burning bodies in the crematoriums is to see life and history from a new perspective. Elie Wiesel, who believes that the Holocaust demands that we see human and religious history from a fresh point of view, said, "In the beginning was the Holocaust. We must therefore start all over again."[5]

How can we continue to hope that as a civilization, we are progressing to a higher level beyond the generations before us? With the stench of the smoke of Auschwitz still in our noses, it is hard to believe in the concept of civilization. Is it possible to talk of a God of love and compassion when there was no divine intervention while more than one and a half million children were starved, tortured, and murdered in the Creator's sight? Can there be a viable belief in a personal God when six million of God's chosen people were led to slaughter and God remained silent? Reeve Robert Brenner polled a thousand Israeli Holocaust survivors to find to what degree their religious beliefs were affected by their death camp experience. His survey disclosed that fifty-three percent of the survivors reported that their camp ordeal modified their belief in God. The survey also revealed that before their imprisonment, fifty-five percent of those questioned had believed in a personal God who was involved in their daily lives. One in four rejected the belief in a personal God after their release from captivity.[6]

When the German theologian Johann-Baptist Metz went to the moral abyss of Auschwitz and stared into its darkness, he stated, "There is no truth for me which I could defend with my back turned toward Auschwitz. There is no sense for me which I could save with my back turned toward Auschwitz. And there is no God to whom I could pray with my back turned toward Auschwitz."[7]

Jewish and Christian theologians have said that our beliefs cannot be the same after the Holocaust. Truth and integrity force us to face Auschwitz and compel us to relinquish some traditional concepts and explanations. One Jewish theologian suggests that our God language has been ruptured and we need new formulations. She says, "Not only did God hang on the gallows with the young boy in *Night (Elie Wiesel's landmark book about the Holocaust)* but the very idea of humanity was incinerated in the Holocaust."[8]

What kind of faith do Christians have if we continue to worship and pray to God as if nothing happened at Auschwitz? Can our liturgical and spiritual lives continue in their present egocentric ethos and never seek to encounter the sheer silence of God at Auschwitz? Are we even sure we are worshipping the Biblical God?

Unfortunately, most American Christians still pray to God with their backs toward Auschwitz. Even our seminaries, our best thinkers, and our church literature rarely, if ever, mention the Holocaust in the context of our understanding of God. The twentieth century's most pregnant God question has occurred, and we have ignored it. Perhaps it is too threatening to our faith to face. Could it be that we already suspect that our current belief in God and our understanding of humankind will be radically shaken if we seriously investigate God's silence at Auschwitz? Do the American churches have the courage and stamina to go to the moral abyss of Auschwitz and seriously confront the hard God questions?

Facing Auschwitz is painful and confusing. It truly is a trial of faith and patience. This book is intended to help the reader to begin to face Auschwitz and to hear its sound of sheer silence. The alternative is to continue to worship a "god" of our own making that may be more of a resemblance to Baal than to the God of Abraham, Isaac, Jacob, and Jesus.

Discussion Questions for
A Sound of Sheer Silence

1. Imagine that you are an American soldier liberating one of the many concentration camps. What would be your thoughts and reactions to the sights you would encounter?

2. Why do some theologians call the Holocaust the most important theological question of the twentieth century?

3. What would motivate or cause an ordinary person to work in a concentration camp and become a part of its dehumanization process and its calculated brutality?

4. How do you interpret Elie Wiesel's quote: "In the beginning was the Holocaust. We must therefore start all over again."

5. What do you think Johann-Baptist Metz meant when he said, "And there is no God to whom I could pray with my back turned toward Auschwitz"?

6. Why do you think the Holocaust challenges some of the treasured Christian doctrines? What would you surmise to be some of those doctrines and beliefs?

2

Why?

Why the Holocaust happened is perhaps one of the most discussed questions surrounding the historical interpretation of this period. The historians, like the sociologists, philosophers, political scientists, and theologians were initially overwhelmed. The magnitude of this premeditated murder is beyond decent human comprehension. The reality is that it did happen to millions of men, women, and children who died horrible deaths because of it.

What follows is not designed to give a comprehensive answer to each suggested cause of the Holocaust projected by many scholars. There are many excellent books that deal with the causes extensively. This discussion is meant to be an introduction to a few of the obvious roots of National Socialism, its anti-Semitic policies and the eventual "Final Solution."

The first and the most apparent root cause of the Holocaust can be found in the implicit and explicit teaching of anti-Semitism by the Christian church through the centuries. Religious enmity with the Jews was a central issue with Christian thinking from the beginning. After the death of Jesus, his followers continued to be practicing Jews. What set them apart as a sect within Judaism was their insistence that Jesus was the Messiah. Their experience with Jesus imbued these Jewish-Christians with an enthusiasm for converting more Jews to accept Jesus of Nazareth as the Messiah. At first, there was a nervous wait and see attitude among the Jewish leadership. Soon conflicting beliefs created controversy in both Jewish and Christian communities. The argument over whether converts had to first become Jewish before they could be Christians was soon center stage. The intensity of the debate increased as Paul and Barnabas brought more gentiles into the Christian communities.

Peter initially came out in favor of admitting gentiles without their first becoming Jews. Peter, Paul, and Barnabas made their case for admitting gentiles into the faith before the Council in Jerusalem. The experiences of the three men persuaded the Apostles and elders to agree with them.

The result of the Jerusalem decision sent Paul and others further into the gentile world and the Church began to grow rapidly. It was not long before the gentiles outnumbered the Jewish Christians. In 70 C.E.(*the initials C.E. stand for the Common Era and has replaced A.D.*), the Romans invaded Jerusalem and destroyed the Temple. From that time on, Jewish-Christian relationships changed. Prior to the destruction of the Temple, the Church was presided over by Jewish leadership. After 70 C.E., the spiritual center of the Church moved west, and eventually located in Rome, and divested itself of Jewish leadership.

Theological anti-Semitism began when the population base of the early Church shifted from being primarily Jewish to a gentile base. The gentiles coming into the Church were from different cultures and backgrounds. They rejected the implied authority of the historic sacred events of Jewish history in favor of their own values and cultures. The Church was becoming Hellenistic and not Jewish.

It was during this period that theological anti-Semitism began to rear its ugly head, and the split between Church and Synagogue increased. The early Christians began teaching that the fall of Jerusalem and the destruction of the Temple was God's anger being laid upon the Jews for rejecting Jesus as the Messiah and for having him crucified. Many Biblical scholars believe that the writers of the four gospels emphasized, for political reasons, that the Jews killed Jesus and played down the fact that it was the Romans who killed him. They were seeking some accommodation with Rome in order to prevent persecution. They wanted to distance themselves from the defeat of the Jewish zealots who caused the war with Rome that resulted in the occupation of Jerusalem and the destruction of the Temple.

Politically, it was a safer course to steer to blame Jesus' death upon the Jews rather than the Romans. As a result all four of the gospels agree on certain points: that Jerusalem was sacked; the Temple was destroyed; thousands of Jews were killed and exiled; this happened because the Roman Army was an instrument of God's anger at the Jews for having rejected and killed Jesus.

The Apostle Paul's first letter to the Thessalonians provides us an example of the early Church's desire to blame the death of Jesus on the Jews. "For you brothers and sisters, became imitators of the churches of God in Christ Jesus that are in Judea, for you suffered the same things from your own compatriots as they did from the Jews, who killed both the Lord Jesus and the prophets, and drove us out; they displease God and oppose everyone by hindering us from speaking to the Gentiles so that they may be saved. Thus they have constantly been filling up the measure of their sins; but God's wrath has overtaken them at last." *(1 Thessalonians 2:14-16)* NRSV.

This anti-Judaic message became one of the major tenets of the Church's teachings about Judaism. The insistence that Jews were responsible for the rejection and death of Jesus was a Church teaching throughout the centuries. In the Church's eyes the Jews were guilty of deicide *(the murder of God)*, an unpardonable crime. The Jews not only killed Jesus, they also rejected him as the Messiah, giving up any right to be God's people. They had denied the New Covenant. Christianity now superseded Judaism as the "New Israel," while Judaism, in this line of thought, had lost its validity. This point of view is called the *supersessionist theory*. The Reverend Michael McGarry explains this theory in his book *Christology After Auschwitz*. Under this concept the Christian church became the fulfillment of Israel's historic mission, and Israel's role in salvation history was over. As a result of this theory, Christians claimed that Jews had lost their election, and were no longer God's chosen people. Their denial of Jesus as the Messiah and the ensuing New Covenant cost Jews their spiritual right to existence. Israel was now a cursed nation and its people were cursed as well. Although the supersessionist theory cannot be found in the New Testament, it has been taught as a Biblical truth for centuries, and many theologians consider it to be the bedrock of Christian anti-Semitism.

Most of the early Church no longer judged Judaism as a valid religion, and viewed its continuance as a threat and a heresy. Some groups and churches in Christian history have gone so far as to claim that the Old Testament has no meaning or importance for Christians. Others have said that the God of the Old Testament was not an accurate image or correct presentation of God. In any case, a religion based on the Old Testament was to be rejected or at best, suspect.

This legacy of anti-Judaism produced numerous anti-Semitic tracts by the early Church fathers, such as Ignatius of Antioch, Cyprian, and perhaps the most vicious against the Jews, Chrysostom. Certainly, sixteen centuries later, the anti-Semitic utterances of Martin Luther were the fruit of more than a thousand years of the Church's teachings about the Jews. Because of the early struggle between Judaism and Christianity that is reflected both in the Epistles of the New Testament, as well as in the Gospels, these passages have evolved into the proof texts for the anti-Semitic sentiments taught by the Church.

One classic example is the parable of the wicked tenants found in *Matthew 21:33-43*. The owner of the vineyard in the "season of fruit" sent a number of his servants to collect his due and they were beaten, killed or stoned by the wicked tenants. He sent others and they suffered a similar fate. Finally he sent his son believing they would respect him. When the son came, the wicked tenants took him and killed him. The text of Matthew has Jesus asking his listeners what the owner will do to the wicked tenants when he comes. They answer Jesus by saying that the owner would put those wicked people to a miserable death and let the vineyard be tended by other tenants who will give him his fruits at the appropriate time. Jesus responds by quoting *Psalm 118:22-23*: "The stone that the builders rejected has become the cornerstone; this was the Lord's doing, and it is amazing in our eyes. Therefore I tell you, the kingdom of God will be taken away from you and given to a people that produces the fruits of the kingdom."

The early Church read this as clearly a parable against the Jews. The son of the owner in the parable was of course to be seen as Jesus. Furthermore since it was the Jews who killed Jesus, God has taken away their spiritual vineyard and given it to the new tenants, the Christians. The parable was and still is interpreted by many as an anti-Judaic teaching. Many New Testament scholars do not believe Jesus actually said the words attributed to him in verses 40,42, and 43. They believe these were added by later Christian storytellers to make the parable an allegory of the rejection of Jesus by the Jews. This parable, and passages such as *Acts 4:5-12 and 1 Peter 2:4-10*, produced the grist for the anti-Judaism mill of the early Church.

There is another facet of the anti-Judaism taught by the Church that needs to be examined. It is known as the Christological lie. The lie was encouraged by Christians through the centuries to assert that Jesus was not a Jew. He may have been born a Jew, but in truth, he never was a Jew. For those not convinced by that piece of distortion, the resurrection provided an even more elaborate rationale for the lie. Even if Jesus were Jewish, after the resurrection, he was no longer Jewish. He left as a Jew, but he was resurrected a non-Jew. This premise gave support for the last part of the lie: Jesus did not die and rise from the dead to save Jews, but he came to take away from them the covenant with God they had not honored.

Regrettably, it must be said that from the beginning, the Church pinned a yellow Star of David on every Jew. The next twenty centuries of anti-Judaic teachings by the Church became the soil out of which a virulent anti-Semitism grew.

National Socialism at its root was anti-Christian, but it used the Church and its anti-Semitic teachings, Protestant and Roman Catholic alike, with great success. While some German Christians were concerned about the encroachment of the Nazi government into the affairs of the Church, they were not overly alarmed or concerned about the persecution of the Jews. Most German Christians had been conditioned to accept Jewish persecution as part of God's ongoing punishment. Dr. A. Roy Eckardt tells of two Christian bishops who visited Adolf Hitler in April of 1933, and asked him what he intended to do about the Jews. Hitler replied that he would do to them precisely what Christian teaching and preaching had been saying for almost two thousand years.[9] Anti-Semitism was so much a part of the German Christian mind set that for many, even their belief in the love of God had no power or influence on them. The silence of the Protestant and Roman Churches, both in and out of Germany, suggests how deep anti-Judaism ran in Christian thought. The apparent silence of Pope Pius XII before and during the Holocaust has become a symbol for the Christian Church's complicity in the horrors of Auschwitz.

Pius XII has become the symbol of the Church's less than heroic stance toward the persecution, deportation, and extermination of the Jews, because both Protestant and Roman Catholic churches pursued courses of action that left indelible stains on their integrity and on Christianity in general. The Pope, being the most visible leader in all of Christianity during the Holocaust, has also become the synonym for the Church's silence.

In recent years some Roman Catholic scholars have written to modify the harsh criticism leveled at Pope Pius XII by other historians and theologians. Their plea, which has its own merit, is that at that point in time, the Pope's primary concern and obligation was the welfare of Roman Catholic Church. He felt obliged by his office, according to the scholars, to keep the Vatican neutral and to keep the churches open and free from persecution and closure, at all costs. They also point out that the Vatican, on a number of occasions, used its influence to attempt to modify Jewish deportation orders in various occupied countries. How enthusiastically these efforts were pursued is still a matter for debate.

In 1942, when all the Allied countries became aware of the Nazis' plans for exterminating the Jews, a great deal of pressure was brought to bear on Pius XII to openly and emphatically denounce the German treatment of the Jews. The Pope, in his Christmas radio message of 1942, gave only a veiled reference to those who were killed or dying solely because of their race. But as had been his custom, Pious XII never mentioned the Jews by name.

In a very broad definition of silent, it would be untrue to say that Pius XII was "silent" about the destruction of the Jews. However, it would be accurate to assert that the Pope was silent because he never publicly came out and condemned the Germans for their treatment of the Jews during the war years. Paul Hillberg has written, "In the multitude of documents published by the Vatican about the diplomatic activity of the Pope and his envoys, the nuncios, there are very few instructions to raise the subject of the Jews. When nuncios spoke, they seem to have followed their own dictates."[10] Hillberg, using documents from the Nuremberg trials, reports that Ernst Von Weizsacher, the German envoy to the Vatican, mentions that he was surprised at the failure of the Pope to say anything about the deportations of over a thousand Jews in Rome. Weizsacker also reported that there was only an indistinct report in the Vatican newspaper, *Osservatore Romano,* after the deportations had literally taken place "under the windows of the Pope." The Jewish section was on the same side of the Tiber River as the Vatican, within a short walking distance.[11] John Cornwell in his book, *Hitler's Pope: The Secret History of Pius XII,* was more direct when he writes, "The failure to utter a candid word about the Final Solution in progress proclaimed to the world that the Vicar of Christ was not moved by pity and anger. From this point of view he was the ideal Pope for Hitler's unspeakable plan. He was Hitler's pawn. He was Hitler's Pope."[12]

Many scholars have pointed out that the Papal diplomacy of this period is to be seen as very reserved, in light of what the Pope felt was his primary obligation to protect the Church from persecution and remain neutral. "The...conclusion is that Pius' commitment to a "diplomatic" church model flowing in large measure from his desire not only to preserve the Church as institution but also to ensure continuation of the conservative social order he and his circle deemed essential for Catholicism's well-being played an absolute critical role in conditioning his response to the plight of the Jews, Poles and other Nazi victim groups."[13]

The public passive stance of the Vatican toward the persecution and extermination of the Jews suggests another principle at work that could also be seen in Protestant churches in other occupied nations as their response to the awareness of the extermination of Jews being carried out by the Germans. Helen Fein, in her impressive work in *Accounting For Genocide,* asserts: "During previous research on the justification of collective violence, I observed the collective (or common) conscience is defined by the boundaries of obligation—that circle of persons toward whom obligations are owed, to whom the rules apply, and whose injuries call for expiation by the community."[14] Using her definition, it would appear that for that time in history, the Vatican and Protestant Churches in central Europe considered Jews to be outside their universe of moral obligation. Her research also suggests that where pre-war anti-Semitic movements and sentiments were strong, there are little if any protests from the church or its leadership over the persecution and deportation of the Jews.[15] Slovakia, the first German-established satellite, was also the first state to agree to export all of its Jews. Slovakia had a strong anti-Semitic movement prior to the war.

Professor Irving Greenberg tells of an incident that reflects the deep-seated anti-Semitism in Slovakia and in the Church. A Rebbe *(a Rabbi or spiritual leader, especially of the Hasidic sect)* of Nietra went in 1942 to Archbishop Kametko of Nietra for the purpose of asking for his intervention against the deportation of the Slovakian Jews. Monsignor Tiso, the head of the Slovakian government, had been the Archbishop's secretary for many years. The Rebbe hoped that the Archbishop would intercede with Tiso and stop the deportation of the Jews. At that point, the Rebbe did not know, that the ultimate destination of the deportations was the gas chamber. He was concerned for the welfare of the elderly, women, and children and he stressed the dangers of hunger and disease. The Archbishop replied to the Rebbe: "It is not just a matter of deportation. You will not die there of hunger and disease. They will slaughter all of you there, old and young alike, women and children, at once. It is the punishment that you deserve for the death of our Lord and Redeemer, Jesus Christ—you have only one solution. Come over to our religion and I will work to annul this decree."[16] If any reconciliation is to take place between Christian and Jew, the Church must accept that it had a part in the construction and operation of Auschwitz.

A second root cause of the Holocaust is to be found in the area of social and intellectual history of Western civilization. Two Christian theologians have written that the racism, sexism, and crude biologism of the Nazis' found its formulation in Aristotelian philosophy and its adoption into Christian theology.[17] In order to have a rationale for the exclusion of freeborn women and slaves from full citizenship, Aristotle argued that the "natures" of women and slaves were different from that of freeborn propertied men. Indeed their "natures" were inferior to such men. Because of their inferior "natures" they must be held in a place of subservience. To allow these "sub-humans" full freedom would threaten the welfare and order of the state.

Adopting the Aristotelian position and moving it into Christian theology, the Church has promulgated a world-view that sought to make inferior the status of women, slaves, and non-whites as a God inspired design. It later became part of the rationalization of the Western colonial powers, as they sought to justify their racist colonial policies with evolutionary and theological concepts. These concepts purported to prove that the European male, specifically, and European Civilization, in particular, were the highest developments of humanity in the long evolutionary process of humankind. Their political expansion was justified, in part, on these racial-theological-evolutionary grounds and it gave rise to a general belief in Western society that women, dark skin races, and certain groups of humans are sub-human. The legitimization of this rationalization of dehumanization became the basis for the Nazis' racial purity programs. We would have had to look hard at the Church during those times to find any serious objections to these ideas.

Another factor was the evolving belief in the ability of humans to have absolute authority and power. Throughout the nineteenth and into the twentieth century, religion had less and less influence on the affairs of nations and human beings. More and more politicians and leaders of the industrial nations had less than serious concerns about divine intervention into the affairs of state. Many wars and terrible events had taken place, but there had been no divine intervention on behalf of one side or the other.

It was soon theorized that if the socio-economic environment, the new technology in service to the state, and a plan for racial purity could be controlled, then it would be possible to develop a race of human beings superior to all others. The plan to create a "new person" and the resulting master race was employed by the Nazis. Armed with an amoral ethos, the Nazis believed they could reshape human society and even the individual. To create a master race, all undesirables would have to be eliminated. This included, the old, the mentally handicapped, the deformed, and homosexuals. Entire groups of people were on the sub-human list such as Gypsies and Slavs, and were marked for elimination. The Jews were at the top of the list of the sub-human groups. The Nazis called the Jews "bacillus," inferring they were the destructive bacteria of society that must be eradicated if the Aryan people were to ever reach their potential.

Value-free science and objectivity had by this time become the altars at which modern humankind was worshipping. And why not? They had provided such giant leaps in knowledge and standards of living for Western civilization. Value-free science and true objectivity had unleashed great power and rewards, but at the expense of serious moral and ethical considerations. Professor Irving Greenberg has stated that science and technology, the laurel leaves of modern man, now converged in the factories of death in the Holocaust. What could be a force for the improvement and betterment of humankind now became the rationale and mechanism for a bureaucratic and technological program for mass murder.

In the absence of strong moral value systems, or the voices to proclaim it, society, by default, gives its moral authority to those in power. Authority that defines its own limits becomes absolute even over God, particularly when there is no fear of God or God's people. This is the path that allowed the National Socialists to have ultimate power over Germany. The value systems of the Churches and of the intellectuals and professionals were tragically silent in the midst of the Nazis ideological take over.

Three historical events dramatize the moral silence of the German society under Hitler. On April 1, 1933, a nationwide boycott of all Jewish owned businesses was ordered by the Nazis. This was followed in six days by the promulgating of the infamous "Aryan" laws. These laws excluded "non-Aryans" from government employment. They caused all Jewish civil servants, university professors, and teachers to be fired from their positions. A month later, orders were given that all books written by Jews or political opponents of the Third Reich and other unacceptable books be burned at large public rallies held all across Germany. There was no large outcry from any major groups or institutions, including the Church when these events took place.

Perhaps the most telling episode took place on November 9, 1938. On the evening of that day, an event took place in Germany that was to be known as *Kristallnacht.* It means the "night of glass" because, on that fateful evening, glass from the windows of synagogues, Jewish businesses, and homes filled the streets of Germany. Thousands of Germans went on a rampage, with the encouragement of the government, to destroy and pillage Jewish synagogues and businesses. As the smoke of their burned buildings drifted into the November night, no Jew could believe he or she had a future in Germany. Shortly after *Kristallnacht,* over 25,000 Jews were sent to concentration camps, and in the months following, approximately one half of Jewish deaths reported in Germany were by suicide.

When the rest of the world heard of *Kristallnacht,* some church groups in other countries protested to the Nazis government. In Germany however, there was absolute silence from all the churches, both Protestant and Roman Catholic. A few months later, the Roman Catholic Church in Germany directed all their churches to honor Adolf Hitler on his fiftieth birthday by having special Masses to implore God's blessings on him.

Professor John Pawlikowski suggests that the Nazis understood the processes of modern humankind. They were aware that the twentieth century provided an opportunity for the uses of human power never seen before in history and that power was in their grasp. In the Nazis' perception, the possibility now existed to reshape human society, and perhaps humanity itself, to an extent never previously imagined. A belief in God's wrath or intervention into the affairs of humans had been rejected by the Nazis early on. They were prepared to rid humankind of the "polluters" of authentic humanity. Mass murder was now to become an official policy for solving societal problems.[18]

When we look through the barbed wire of Auschwitz, we see an assembly line of death put together in part by unrestrained human freedom, modern technology, and the belief that some humans were superior to others, while other human beings were not fully human at all. There was no power, transcendent or worldly, that could keep the Third Reich from carrying out their plans. The Jew was to feel the full fury of this belief. Millions of Jewish men, women, and children, were to be dehumanized to the point they had no name, only a number tattooed on their flesh.

When we face Auschwitz we see the fire and billows of smoke from the furnaces throwing not only the incinerated ashes of Jews to the wind, but also the ashes of Christian integrity. Unless we accept that fact and begin to deal with it, we have truly turned our backs to Auschwitz and to God.

Discussion Questions for
Why?

1. Why is anti-Semitism still an issue in our country? In the world? In some churches?

2. Can you explain the supersessionist theory? Were you ever exposed to this teaching?

3. What are your feelings about the "silence" of the churches in Germany during the Holocaust? What part do you think patriotism played in their silence? Can patriotism become a secular god we worship?

4. Professor Fein talks about "boundaries of obligation" for those who are accepted by the community. Those within the boundaries are protected or at least given the protection of the law. Jews, Gypsies, homosexuals, and the mentally impaired were considered outside the boundaries in Nazi Germany. Do we have boundaries in our society? If so how do we overcome them?

3

In the Presence
of
Burning Children

Standing at the barbed wire of Auschwitz and gazing inside, we cannot limit our vision to the drab barracks, the gas chambers, or the crematoriums. We must see the victims themselves, not as nameless bodies stacked in piles like wood in old black and white photographs or as cold nameless statistics. We must look into their eyes, and somehow let their humanness resonate with ours. Unless the human dimension becomes real for us, Auschwitz will never be more than another footnote in the long history of human cruelty.

Professor Irving Greenberg, writing in an article, quoted from the transcript of a Polish guard assigned to Auschwitz. The guard testified at the Nuremburg trial that women who were carrying children were always sent to the crematorium. The reason was because the children had no labor value and unless the mothers went along, there was the possibility that separating them would cause panic or hysteria. The children were wrestled from their parents outside the crematorium and sent to the gas chambers separately. To crowd as many as possible into the gas chambers was the urgent consideration. Separating the children meant that more could be packed in or they could be thrown in over the heads of adults, once the chamber was full. Then, the guard made an unthinkable statement. He revealed that at the height of the extermination of the Jews in 1944, orders were issued for children to be thrown straight into the crematorium furnaces, or into a burning pit near the crematorium, without being gassed first.

The Russian prosecutor responded with disbelief. He wanted to know whether the children were thrown into the fire alive, or were they killed first. The guard replied that they were thrown in alive and that their screams could be heard all over the camp.[19]

In response to that story as well as thousands of others, Professor Greenberg made this comment concerning the Holocaust: "No statement, theological or otherwise, should be made that would not be credible in the presence of burning children."[20] Easy answers to Auschwitz do not take burning children seriously.

One way to become serious about the meaning of Auschwitz is to discover what happened to individual victims. To be drawn into the suffering and agony they had to undergo, is to give flesh and bone to the cold statistics of the Holocaust. To put the succeeding stories and incidents into perspective, the thoughts of Elie Wiesel are appropriate. Speaking on the horror of the Holocaust, Wiesel says that what the Germans were really trying to do was to exterminate the Jews not only physically but also spiritually. It was by design that the Nazis debased, defamed, and attempted to remove all moral values from the Jews. It was a calculated process of total dehumanization. The language of the camps was obscene and the words used to describe the Jews were all inhuman. Life in the death camps was totally dependent upon the wishes and whims of German authority. Any guard could wantonly beat or kill a Jewish prisoner without fear of any disciplinary action. They had absolute authority with the power of life and death over their helpless prisoners. Indeed, they sought to substitute themselves for the Jewish God.[21]

Terrence Des Pres in his book *The Survivor: An Anatomy of Life in The Death Camps*, describes the Nazis dehumanization program as the "excremental assault."[22] The program began when the Jews were herded on the railroad boxcars like animals and packed so tightly that they were forced to stand. Unable to move to any degree, it was impossible for them to urinate or defecate except in their own clothing as they stood. A journey to a death camp could take several days. Upon arriving at the camp the "excremental assault" continued. In most camps, the prisoners could only go to the latrine at specified times. Going to the toilet at any other time could mean severe beatings or even death. To make the situation even worse, the food or soup given to the prisoners was of such poor quality as to cause diarrhea and dysentery. In such cases, they were forced to eliminate in their eating utensils or in their clothing.

The prisoners were treated in ways that were calculated to dehumanize them, not only in the eyes of their captors, but also in their own eyes. The whole process was contrived to fill the prisoners with such deep self-contempt that they no longer had the will to live. Some prisoners were so dehumanized by the brutal system, they became known as the *Muselmanns*. Such a person was dead while still alive. Whatever spark of human life there had been was now snuffed out. They plodded off to work in silence and were too empty of emotions to feel anything. Primo Levi described the *Muselmann* in these words: "One hesitates to call them living; one hesitates to call their death death, in the face of which they have no fear, as they are too tired to understand."[23]

When the Jews of Eastern Europe were rounded up by the Germans and placed in ghettos, it was apparent to them how cruel the Nazis could be. In the beginning, most of the Jews gathered in the ghettos were unaware that the Resettlement Operations, which were publicized as programs for resettling Jews in other parts of the country, were only covers for deportation to the death camps. Alexander Donat recorded with vivid clarity many of the tragic events of the Warsaw ghetto. He told of a young mother who ran out of her apartment into the street to get milk for her baby. Her husband had left for work earlier in the morning. In her haste to get milk for her baby the young mother was dressed only in her bathrobe and slippers. As she ran toward the store where she purchased her milk, she ran into one of the Resettlement Operations. When she was unable to produce the proper documents, in spite of protesting vehemently that she possessed them, she was seized and dragged toward a high-boarded wagon. She pleaded with them about her baby left alone in the apartment, but they ignored her. It was apparent to her that they intended to take her away, and she suddenly pulled herself loose from the guards' grips. As she bolted away, four guards pounced on her, hitting her and throwing her to the ground. They picked her up and threw her into the wagon. Donat said he could hear her screams of despair and anguish as the wagon moved away.[24]

On September 23, 1942, the ghetto at Stolpce, Poland was surrounded by German troops. Execution trenches had been dug outside the town in preparation of the mass killings. The Germans marched into the ghetto, searching all the houses, apartments, and buildings. Eliezer Melamed, who survived, told how he and his girl friend hid in a room behind some sacks of flour. A mother and her three children followed them into the room. The children hid in the corner of the room and the mother sought to conceal herself in another room.

When the German soldiers entered, they discovered the children. As they were being taken out of their hiding place, one of the children, a small boy began to cry out for his "Mama!" One of the other boys told his brother in Yiddish to shut up, or they would take her, too. The young boy stopped crying and the mother remained hidden and silent. Her children were taken out and she never saw them again. After they were gone, the mother, in great anguish and pain, hit her head on the wall over and over again.[25]

Those Jews, who were not exterminated outside their towns or ghettos, faced the excruciating train trip to the death camps. They were packed onto cattle and boxcars so tightly that it was impossible to sit or lie down. It is no wonder that with no sanitary facilities in the boxcars, no water, no food, no heat in winter, and in most cases very little fresh air, many of the passengers, especially the very young, old, and sick, died en route to the camps.

Many thousands of Jews were deported from Kielce, Poland to Treblinka on August 24, 1942. The trip to Treblinka normally took only three hours but on this occasion it took nearly twenty-four hours. Many of those in the train cars fainted from heat, hunger, thirst, and exhaustion. Hundreds of others died of suffocation. Large numbers drank their own urine to try to avoid dehydration. One survivor reported that nearly one third of the train was dead upon arrival at Treblinka.[26]

The dehumanization process was well on its way by the time the trains reached the camps. The process was accelerated once the victims arrived at the unloading areas. They were ordered off the trains to the accompaniment of shouts and whips. The men and women were separated and occasionally, the women were sent directly to the undressing barracks where they were forced to strip completely. Small children were usually allowed to accompany their mothers. The usual practice was for men and women to march past a medical officer who pointed left or right in a ritual euphemistically called a "selection". Those who were sent to the left, for example, were headed for the gas chambers, although they were unaware of the significance at the time. Those sent to the right were to be used as laborers until they were worked to death or died of disease, malnutrition, or another selection.[27]

Those doomed to the gas chambers, both men and women, were sent to the undressing barracks. The women were next sent to the "beauty parlor" where all their hair was cut off. Hair was sent to Germany to be used in upholstery and insulation products. Women were also subjected to searches of their vaginal and rectal areas, to look for jewelry or gold that might be hidden away. From the undressing barracks, both the men and the women were forced to run naked in segregated groups down a tree-lined path to the gas chambers. They were often compelled to make this run under the lashes of the camp guards and the SS. The men were usually the first to be sent to the "showers," and then the women, followed by the children.

One of the hundreds of thousands of heart wrenching stories about the initial selection after disembarking from the trains comes from Olga Lengyel. As the selections were being made, she and her mother were directed over to an adult group. Her youngest son was sent to where the children were standing along with the old people. Then, the officer asked her oldest son if he was over twelve years old. Olga intervened, saying that he was not yet twelve, he just looked older. So the officer pointed him to the left. Then she persuaded her mother to go with the children. In her mind she was attempting to spare them both from hard labor. Unwittingly, she sent them both to the gas chamber.[28]

After those who had been packed into a gas chamber were dead, a work group of Jewish prisoners was sent inside to remove all the bodies. If the victims had not been searched or had their head shaved before they were gassed, this work group was assigned the gruesome task. Some in the work group were called "Dentists" because their task was to use a pair of pliers or a hammer to remove all the gold teeth and crowns from the victims. One survivor told of laboring in such a work group, and was assigned the task of shaving the hair off the dead women. In one load of women's bodies brought to him for shaving was the body of his wife and he was forced to shave her hair.[29]

Part of the hell that made up the environment of the death camps, was not knowing when you would be beaten, tortured, or killed. There was no rationale to protect the prisoner from any obscenity. Rudolf Reder, one of only two survivors of the Belzac extermination camp in Poland, wrote about an incident that dramatizes the hellish-like existence to which the inmates were subjected. He reported that a very young healthy boy was selected to work at the camp. He possessed a cheerful and positive countenance and one day he innocently asked if anyone had escaped from Belzac. A guard overheard him and they took him and tortured him to death. He was first stripped naked and taken to a gallows where he was hung upside down. He was healthy and did not die, so they took him down from the gallows and stretched him out on the ground and poked sand down his throat with sticks until he was dead.[30]

If there is one thing that underscores the total evil and obscenity of the Holocaust, it is the way the Germans treated children, especially the babies. Samuel Rajzman a survivor of Treblinka gave testimony at the Nuremberg Tribunal of what happened in that death camp. He testified that because little babies at their mother's breast held up the processing, especially the head shaving, it was decided that the babies would be separated from their mothers when they got off the train. The children were taken to a very large trench. When a substantial number had been collected, they were shot and thrown into the fire. They did not bother to see if the children were dead or not, and often, it was possible to hear their cries of anguish in the fire.[31]

How can we keep staring through the barbed wire of Auschwitz and not look such horror in the eye? The answer for most American Christians is that we really have not. Indeed it seems almost a national resolve not to face Auschwitz, or deal with is spiritual implications, even by the vast majority of Christians in this country. Many scholars, both Jewish and Christian, have tried to raise the theological questions posed by the Holocaust, but with very little success beyond academia.

As we look into the faces of the victims of Auschwitz who were tortured, abused, and dehumanized, we must, along with them, ask about our relationship with God. Andre L. Stein, who was a survivor of the Holocaust, wrote about the feelings of other survivors: "For many…language is further reduced to one single question: Where is God?"[32]

The Jewish author Ka-tzetnik, a Holocaust survivor, provides us with a poignant conclusion to this chapter in his book *Star Eternal*. He returns in prose to Park Street, the first Polish street taken by the invading Germans in September 1939. And now, as he looks upon Park Street, everything he knew is gone. The cradle in which he slept is gone, as is the mother who so tenderly rocked it. His sisters golden hair, that his mother so lovingly brushed is somewhere in Germany in a piece of upholstery. The huge piles of shoes removed from Auschwitz victims are all that remain of tens of thousands of helpless victims. One pair of those shoes is his father's. "Hair, shoes, mother, sister, father—more words that can never be the same…. Yet one longs for something. Not money, but maybe a strand of hair or a shoe would help, or even "a broken wheel from my little brother's skates; a mote of dust that on my mother rested—."[33]

Discussion Questions for
In the Presence of Burning Children

1. "No statement, theological or otherwise, should be made that would not be credible in the presence of burning children." What is your response to Professor Irving Greenberg's statement concerning comments about the Holocaust?

2. The dehumanization process used by the Nazis enabled them to control, abuse, and annihilate Jews. Do you think dehumanization is also at the root of racism in our country? Have we used it against our wartime enemies in the past? Which comes first hate, or dehumanization?

3. Many wonder why so many "good" Germans went along with the Nazis and their persecution of Jews. What do you think was the reason?

4. Can you imagine what it was like to be a Jew in Hitler's Germany? To be a prisoner in a concentration camp? How would you describe your feelings?

5. How would you feel as a German Jew if you knew all the churches in your country and a large portion of the world did not care about your persecution or the death camps?

4

The Silence of God

The Holocaust has been called the most important God question of the twentieth century. Where was God during the horror and devastation? Why did God not answer the prayers for deliverance of the chosen people of Israel? Why would God, who has been characterized for centuries as loving, merciful, and loyal to the children of Abraham, Isaac, and Jacob, allow over six million of them to be murdered in the most inhumane of ways? Where was God when live children were tossed into the burning pits? "Why, God, why?" was a cry that came from the lips of countless numbers of victims of the Holocaust as well as from the survivors and it continues today from any theologically sensitive person who studies the story of Auschwitz.

When we peer across the barbed wire of Auschwitz and see the smoke, and smell the burning flesh of millions of Jews and other human beings, we are taxed to find evidence of God's presence there. Indeed, many inmates of Auschwitz and other death camps came to the same conclusion.

Elie Wiesel in *Night* tells the story of a rabbi from a small Polish community. He was old and stooped and his lips trembled. "He used to pray all the time, in the block, in the yard, in the ranks. He would recite whole pages of the Talmud from memory, argue with himself, ask himself questions and answer himself. And one day he said to me: 'It's the end. God is no longer with us.'

And as though he had repented of having spoken such words, so clipped, so cold, he added in his faint voice:

'I know. One has no right to say things like that. I know. Man is too small, too humble and inconsiderable to seek to understand the mysterious ways of God. But what can I do? I'm not a sage, one of the elect, nor a saint. I'm just an ordinary creature of flesh and blood. I've got eyes too, and I can see what they're doing here. Where is divine mercy? Where is God? How can I believe, how could anyone believe, in this merciful God?'"[34]

This episode from *Night*, in microcosm, exhibits in bold relief some of the theological questions that arise from the serious study of the Holocaust. Both Jewish and Christian theologians have sought to deal with these questions. As could be expected, their answers can be found all over the theological spectrum. With the exception of the very conservative theologians, Auschwitz brings into question all the pronouncements by both Jews and Christians on the nature of God. For some the very existence of God is in question. Many victims of the death camps had reason to doubt the existence of God. One survivor said, "...I refuse to believe God is a horrible sadist. There are no other choices at all. God either does not exist or He is the Devil. I'd simply prefer to believe in no God at all."[35]

One survivor saw the Holocaust as a stupendous test. "Now when man writes his history he can say there was a vast laboratory experiment conducted by man during the 1940's to see if there is a God or not. The conclusion was no God exists."[36]

In *The Sunflower* Simon Wiesenthal says, "In a concentration camp...one begins to doubt, one begins to cease to believe in a world order in which God has a definite place. One really begins to think that God is on leave. Otherwise the present state of things wouldn't be possible. God must be away. And he has no deputy."[37]

The attempt to explain God's absence or silence during the Holocaust has necessitated many theologians to move across the boundaries of conventional doctrine. Any serious study of the Holocaust will force a redefinition of providence and prayer. Does God really hear and answer prayer? If so, why were the prayers for deliverance of six million of God's people left unanswered? Millions of Jews left the freight cars and entered the gas chambers either singing or reciting the prayer called the *Ani-Ma-amin*: "I affirm, with unbroken firmness, that the Messiah will come. And even though He tarries, even so, I affirm it."

Obviously, from the Jewish perspective, the Messiah did not come and has not come. This observation raises some troubling questions for Christians. Robert McAfee Brown made this observation: "The Jew laments: 'Since the world is so evil, why does the Messiah not come?' The Christian wonders: 'Why, since the Messiah has come, does the world remain so evil?'"[38]

Given our traditional teachings on the nature and character of God these questions are indeed bothersome. The Holocaust has shown that the prayers for deliverance from both Christian and Jew appear to have been unanswered. A more fearful question is raised: Does God answer prayer at all? If God would not intervene and remained silent while over one million, five hundred thousand innocent children were brutalized, and some thrown into pits of fire while still alive, is such a God worthy of worship and praise? Can we say beyond a doubt that God is love, while acknowledging there was no divine intervention in the suffering and torture of millions of God's people?

We must be careful not to separate the Christian experience from the Jewish experience. Unless we fall into the immoral arguments of anti-Semitism and supersessionism, we are still faced with the silence of God at Auschwitz.

Johann-Baptist Metz, a German theologian, makes this point: "Let us not say: after all there are for us Christians other God experiences beside Auschwitz. That's true! But if there is no God for us in Auschwitz, how can there be a God anywhere else?"[39]

If doubts are raised about God's hearing and answering prayer, what does God's silence at Auschwitz say about our understanding of the providence of God? As we stand outside the barbed wire of Auschwitz and contemplate the murder of millions and millions of human beings under the most brutal of conditions imaginable, we are hard pressed to continue to believe in the benevolent providence of God.

Indeed, we are pushed to say either God is indifferent or adverse toward what happens to human beings, or God is caring, but respects the freedom of humans. If we opt for God's indifference, we must abandon our belief in God's purposefulness and design for the world. Such a position ultimately would lead us to despair and the rejection of moral values. If, on the other hand we see God as adverse to humankind, we must see that all the good, all the achievements of humans in science, art, literature, compassion, and technology are, in fact, a defeat for an antagonistic God. If we continue to believe God cares about humanity, we must see how this can be, in light of Auschwitz.

This latter position will force us to reject the narcissistic belief that is so prevalent in so many congregations. We cannot believe that the great purpose of the God of the universe is to put a cocoon of love and protection around us and to take care of us. Such a belief would be an obscenity to the victims of Auschwitz and all the other death camps. As Arthur Telyveld states in his book *Atheism Is Dead*: "Most people who affirm that God lives have not emancipated themselves from the juvenile notion that the chief function of God is to take care of them."[40]

When we examine all the events, sorrows, tragedies, and evils of life, we must, by the force of sheer logic, either reject the idea of special providence, or accept the premise that God is a very capricious being. Life is full of risk, accidents, disorder, disease, insanity, violence, failure, and death. To imagine that the God of the universe saved *me* from an accident or found *me* a job is to turn your back on

Auschwitz. We must again recall the soul searching words of Professor Irving Greenberg, "Let us offer this fundamental criterion after the Holocaust. No statement, theological or otherwise, should be made that would not be credible in the presence of burning children."[41] Professor Greenberg gives us a painful plumb line for our ideas about the providence of God. Taken seriously, such a plumb line will force us to rethink a number of our cherished sentimental beliefs. Undoubtedly such a plumb line is capable of causing despair and hopelessness, and it is certain that the victims of Auschwitz felt the sting of such a plumb line. Try as we will to deny the plumb line, we often find that what we believe will not sound credible in the presence of burning children.

How the theologians responded to the Holocaust and its questions about God is instructive. These limited pages do not allow space to go into each theologian in depth without the risk of doing them injustice. However, an attempt is made to capsulate some ideas of a few Jewish and Christian theologians.

In 1965, Rabbi Ignaz Maybaum published *The Face of God After Auschwitz*, and in his book, he affirms that God does intervene in history, particularly in the history of Jews. Maybaum insists that the Holocaust was one of God's most significant interventions. He rejects the idea held by some that the Holocaust was God's punishment of Jews. He maintains that the Holocaust was the Jewish version of the crucifixion of Jesus. Even as Jesus was an innocent sacrificial victim who made possible the salvation of humankind, so the deaths of six million innocent Jews were a sacrifice to the same end. Maybaum asserts that Auschwitz was the Golgotha of modern humanity. His thinking places the Holocaust Jews as sacrificial victims, bringing humankind into the modern world, and he sees God as using Hitler in the same manner as Nebuchadnezzar was used in destroying Jerusalem.[42] It is Maybaum's purpose to affirm the Biblical God of history and the place of Jews as the chosen people. Whatever else is intended, Maybaum sees God as willing to sacrifice six million innocent people to the most hideous of deaths in order to serve a greater divine purpose. Such a view obviously found many detractors.

In 1966, another book was published that took an entirely different view of the Holocaust than did Maybaum's. Rabbi Richard L. Rubenstein wrote *After Auschwitz*, which was a rejection of the Biblical God of election and covenant. Some accused Rubenstein of being an atheist, particularly in light of his comments that suggested we live in the time of the death of God.[43]

Clearly, he saw the plumb line and reacted to it. He states his concern concisely: "How can Jews believe in an omnipotent, beneficent God after Auschwitz? Traditional Jewish theology maintains that God is the ultimate, omnipotent actor in historical drama. It has interpreted every major catastrophe in Jewish history as God's punishment of a sinful Israel. I fail to see how this position can be maintained without regarding Hitler and the SS as instruments of God's will. The agony of European Jewry cannot be likened to the testing of Job. To see any purpose in the death camps, the traditional believer is forced to regard the most demonic, anti-human explosion of all history as a meaningful expression of God's purposes. The idea is simply too obscene for me to accept."[44]

Rubenstein's rejection of the traditional concepts of the Biblical God and covenant election of Jews moved him to further positions regarding Jewish beliefs. He maintained that if Jewish history was aimed at the return of Jews to their homeland, then, for all intents and purposes, Jewish history had come to an end. Accordingly, since Jewish history had come to an end after Auschwitz, so had the God of Israel come to an end. For Rubenstein, the world is a place of pain, suffering, and defeat, and Auschwitz had confirmed this belief. Certainly, from his perspective, there was no intervention from the God of the Old or New Testament.

Needless to say, Rubenstein's views evoked other responses to the plumb line of Auschwitz. One response came from Arthur A. Cohen, a highly regarded Jewish thinker. Unlike Rubenstein, Cohen defended the doctrine of the election of Jews as God's chosen people. That Jews are still here, in spite of the Holocaust, and the fact that the state of Israel exists, are for him, the ultimate proof of Jewish election. Cohen called the Holocaust *"the tremendum"* which conveys the meaning of vastness and terror. He also suggests that tremendum means an impenetrable mystery. He does not accept the view that God has an active role in human history, and thus, does not blame God for the Holocaust. Cohen says that human freedom is absolute; otherwise human beings would be mere robots. His position, at the risk of over simplification, is that God does not interfere with or in human affairs, but serves only as a Teacher of those who consent to be taught. Auschwitz for Cohen was man's doing, not God's.

Another Jewish author, Rabbi Emil L. Fackenheim, rejects the idea that the Holocaust was God's punishment of Jews. He also rejects Maybaum's view that the Holocaust victims were a sacrificial offering. The Holocaust was for him the most disruptive event in the history of the Jewish people. Unlike others who denied God's presence in the Holocaust, Fackenheim says that while God's presence in Auschwitz cannot be confirmed, there was a "commanding Voice" that was heard. The "commanding Voice" dictated a 614th commandment. There are 613 acknowledged commandments in Judaism, and he is suggesting a 614th as a result of the Holocaust. The four parts to the 614th commandment are: 1) Jews are commanded to survive as Jews; 2) Jews are never to forget the victims of the

Holocaust; 3) Jews are forbidden ever to despair of God despite of what happens, for fear Judaism will die; 4) Jews are never to despair that the world will become the kingdom of God or they will be among those who make the world a meaningless place where God is dead. "To abandon any of these imperatives, in response to Hitler's victory at Auschwitz, would be to hand him yet another posthumous victory."[45] Fackenheim's views are generally well received by many Jewish communities because they maintain the distinctive relationship Jews have with God, and also affirm God's presence among God's people suffering in the death camps. His views, deny any complicity of God with the Nazi oppressors. Among his critics there has been concern over his position that the "commanding Voice" has commanded Jews to survive as Jews. "It hardly seemed likely that even a jealous God would require the annihilation of six million Jews as the occasion for a commandment forbidding Jews to permit the demise of their tradition."[46]

For Jewish theologians the plumb line that no theological statement should be made that would not be credible in the presence of burning children still exists, and the debate continues.

The Christian approach to the plumb line of Auschwitz fares no better than the Jewish. Because of the serious and disturbing aspects of the Holocaust, many Christian theologians and church leaders have elected to not face Auschwitz. To face Auschwitz head on is to ask for a reorientation of Christian doctrine, and it forces a serious thinker to give up the juvenile notion that God's sole purpose is to take care of individuals as Telyveld so aptly stated.

Some Christian theologians have had the courage to face Auschwitz and their responses are as varied as those of their Jewish counterparts. Jurgen Moltmann's view in his book, *The Crucified God*, is that God was in Auschwitz and suffered there as he did on the cross. He believes Auschwitz, more than any event in history since the Crucifixion, demonstrates that God saves people, including the Jews. His view is that through the cross, God participated in their suffering and pain. Moltmann believes that humanity and God seem to intersect at the point of human suffering, as they did in the crucifixion of Jesus. The Resurrection showed how the suffering of humankind and God leads to a new level of existence and to salvation.[47]

Critics of Moltmann's theology of the cross argue that there is no way we can say six million Jews were liberated from death or from any other form of suffering through the crucifixion. To compare their suffering to that of Jesus on the cross is to reinterpret the meaning of the crucifixion. The cross, historically in Christian thinking, was a voluntary act carried out by Jesus to achieve the redemption of humankind. Auschwitz was neither voluntary nor redemptive.[48] Moltmann's the-

ology of the cross has support among other theologians but with different emphasis or interpretation.

Franklin Sherman, another Christian theologian, would agree with Moltmann
that the cross teaches us that God does participate in the sufferings of God's people. The Jewish prophetic tradition also taught that God suffered with God's
people. For Sherman, this should be the touchstone of a unity between Christians
and Jews. He would be in the school of thinking that would affirm God's presence in Auschwitz.

One Christian theologian who does not link a theology of the cross with Auschwitz is Gregory Baum. He does not try to connect Auschwitz with the cross
because he sees Auschwitz as the event that forces us to an examination of our
current understanding of the Christ event. His view is that Christianity must
purge itself of all anti-Semitic teachings and endorse the validity of Judaism. He
sees Auschwitz as a "sign of the times" for the church to radically reformulate its
approach to the faith. For Baum, as for others, the plumb line makes it necessary
to reformulate the Christian doctrine of God.

These views of Jewish and Christian theologians are only very brief glimpses
into their thinking, which they have obviously elaborated and explained in
greater detail than has been attempted here. There are, of course, many other
Jewish and Christian theologians who have addressed the God questions of Auschwitz but these questions still remain for each Christian and Jew to answer for
themselves. Where was God? Why was God silent? Does God really intervene
into history? Do prayers have any validity after Auschwitz? It would seem we have
no choice, if we are honest with ourselves, but to reformulate our thinking about
God and God's providence. To ignore the plumb line is to ignore reality.

What kind of theological statement can we make about God that would be
credible in the presence of burning children? Perhaps, as others have suggested,
the question is best answered by asking: "Where was humankind and why was it
silent at Auschwitz?" Arthur Cohen felt Auschwitz was man's doing, not God's.
Elie Wiesel asks the question succinctly: "Where was humankind in Auschwitz?"
John Roth states: "The Holocaust...is human action not God's. It is rooted in
human judgements, not God's. And yet...God still stands trial at Auschwitz."[49]
Reeve Robert Brenner states that the survivors had a persistent theme, and it was
that six million Jews died exclusively because of man's inhumanity to man. As
one survivor observed: "How is it when a man murders another man you never
hear that God is at fault?...A political assassination? Not a word about God? A
terrorist attack killing a number of people? The terrorists are blamed, not God.
But somehow with regard to the death of the six million European Jews, God has

to be dragged in to explain what ought to be explained simply by the fact recurring again and again of the mistreatment by one portion of humanity of another portion of humanity, especially the mistreatment of Jews by others."[50]

Next, the question we must ask is obvious: "Where was humankind during the Holocaust?" The answer to this question is as difficult to comprehend as the question of God's silence. While not as apparent as the silent God question, the silence of humanity also poses a theological question. In the chapter on "Why?" we discussed the part that Christian anti-Semitic heritage played in allowing Auschwitz to happen, but that is not to say that all Christians were or are anti-Semitic, or would have approved of the death camps. Most faithful Christians, even during the Holocaust would on a personal basis be sickened at what was going on. Yet, studies show that a large number of death camp guards and administrators were baptized Christians. Professor Aleksander Lasik of Bydgoszcz, Poland reports in his study of *The Religious Denominations of the Nazi Concentration Camps' Staff: The Examples of KL Auschwitz and KL Stuffhof* that religion did not appear to have much importance to camp staff members.[51] Indeed, the 1940 census in Germany shows that 95 per cent of the German people were affiliated with a church. If Germany were such a Christian body politic, how could the churches have remained so silent about the abuse and treatment of Jews?

Books and international conferences have addressed that very issue. Research has revealed that the churches, both Roman Catholic and Protestant, were conspicuous by their silence. The reasons for their silence are varied. Again at the risk of over-simplification, listed below are some of the reasons for the silence.

One obvious reason for the silence of the churches was the lack of prophetic leadership. Early in 1933, Hitler realized that if he could achieve recognition from the Roman Catholic Church, it would serve him well at home and abroad. Thus when Hitler was approached by Rome for a formal concordat that offered both a legal status to the church, as well as protection for the church and its religious functions, he was amiable, except for some modifications. Hitler's approval depended upon the insertion in the concordat that all Catholics in Germany withdraw from social and political action as Catholics and that the Catholic Center Party be disbanded. The Center Party represented the last democratic political party in Germany.

The concordat was signed in July of 1933. In his book, Cornwell says about the concordat: "Nothing could have been better designed to deliver the powerful institution of the Catholic Church in Germany into the hands of Hitler."[52] From that time on, the only protests that issued forth from Rome were complaints that the Third Reich was violating one or more of its agreements in the concordat. Pope Pious XII's position, as previously stated, was that the welfare and protection of the church was his first priority. The consistent Roman Catholic view was that the church was charged with the salvation of the souls of their followers. That was accomplished by having the Mass and the Sacraments available to their people. Without the Mass and Sacraments, there could be no salvation for the faithful. To attack Hitler and his anti-Semitic Jewish activities would not be in the best interests of the church. Thus, throughout the Holocaust, Rome was publicly silent about the "Jewish situation".

Interestingly enough, when the Roman Catholic Church in Germany did muster enough confidence to oppose Hitler's policies, it met with limited success. In the early years, signs of resistance to the Third Reich did appear. There was opposition to the restrictions that the government had placed on the church's press. A greater sign of resistance came in 1934 when the church was involved in a struggle to maintain their own schools and youth programs. In 1937, the struggle had so escalated that the Roman Catholic school parents were asked to vote if they wanted to remain strictly a religious school or become a community or public school under the guidance of the state. Political and economic realities, being what they were, the church was doomed to lose the vote. The vote was immediately protested as a violation of the concordat. While it is true that the Roman Catholic Church did offer resistance to the Nazis in the early years, it was always directed at the abridgement of the guarantees and spirit of the 1933 concordat; the Jewish problem was never mentioned. Nothing came from the church, even after the infamous *Kristallnacht* of 1938.

Once World War II began in 1939, the whole character of the Roman Catholic Church's relationship to the Third Reich changed. With all the controls over education, media, and institutions that a totalitarian state like Germany could muster, it was all focused on nationalism. The giant Nazi rallies, torch light parades, and appeals to a bruised German pride, all served to stir up the people in a fury of nationalism. One scholar has written: "I submit that one of the main reasons why German Catholicism and its leaders failed to mount an effective resistance to Hitler is to be found in the extent to which those same leaders were themselves caught up in the uncritically nationalistic mood of the time."[53]

The church was also caught up in its own doctrine. That doctrine was simply that Roman Catholic Christians are always obedient to legitimate authority; indeed they must "render unto Caesar". For good and obedient Roman Catholics, imbued with a fierce patriotism for the Fatherland, Hitler, and the Nazis, they were legitimate authority. As the Bishop of Munster said, "Of course we

Christians make no revolution! We will continue to do our duty in obedience to God, out of love for our German Folk and Fatherland."[54] This position precluded any large scale organized resistance or opposition to the Nazis and their policies. Indeed Gordon Zahn in his study concluded, "…if the Nazis had not decided upon an ideological campaign against Christianity…they would have found the Catholic Church and most of it members among the most ardent defenders of the Third Reich."[55] This is not to imply that all Roman Catholic bishops, priests, religious, and laity went along unquestioningly with the Nazis. There were numerous occasions when individual Roman Catholics resisted Nazis policies, aided Jews, spent time in concentration camps and many were executed. The point, however, is that the hierarchy of the German Roman Catholic Church was silent about the Nazis treatment of Jews before and during the Holocaust.

The Protestant churches fare no better under scrutiny than does the Roman Catholic Church. There were some notable exceptions that will be discussed below. The Protestant churches, like their Roman Catholic counterparts, were also swept up in the wave of nationalism that ushered in the Third Reich. Most of Germany's Christians were already predisposed to a position of anti-Semitism. In January of 1933 when Hitler came into power, the Protestant leadership welcomed him. While some small groups, like the Jehovah Witnesses, refused to cooperate with the Nazis, most mainline Protestant churches embraced Hitler, and, in some cases, even revised church doctrines to be in closer harmony with the Nazi party and its aims.

Those Christians and the churches, whose loyalty to the Third Reich and Hitler was unquestioned, became known as the "German Christians." They envisioned Hitler as God's chosen man for Germany. With the help of the Nazis, "German Christians" won the church elections of July of 1933. They elected Ludwig Muller as the first bishop of the Evangelical Reich Church, and he and the "German Christians" soon tried to put an Aryan rule in the church. Such a rule would restrict participation in the life of the church by Jewish Christians. This move created an opposition group that was headed by Martin Niemoller, who later would suffer in concentration camps because of his opposition to Hitler and the Nazis. This small, but articulate, group of opposing clergy would call itself The Confessing Church. In 1934, the Confessing Church numbered approximately 5,000 clergy. That same year, The Confessing Church issued what is known as the Barmen Declaration. The Barmen statement spoke out against state control of the church, for freedom of the Word of God, for the Lordship of Jesus Christ, and indirectly against the "German Christians." Interestingly, nothing was said directly about the Jewish question. The Confessing Church remained a minority, and lost members as pressure was applied by the state. As one historian of the period has said, "Most of the Confessing Church's members warmly endorsed Hitler's aggressive foreign policy and his military victories. None of the church leaders ever led their followers to believe that the Nazi government was unworthy of their support."[56]

One other significant Protestant church was the Lutheran Free Church. This particular Lutheran group had its beginnings in the 1830s when in protest to the forced union of Reformed and Lutheran Churches in Prussia, they seceded from the union, rather than accept Reformed theology and liturgy. They gained official recognition in 1841 and formed the Evangelical Lutheran Free Church in Prussia. Following the Prussian lead, many other strict Lutheran congregations in other areas formed Free Lutheran Synods. By 1900, the Free Lutherans were an association of related, but independent, synods.

During the early years of the twentieth century, the Free Lutherans were opposed to the principles of democracy, and even discouraged their members from joining political parties. They condemned the godlessness of the secular Weimar Republic (*the constitutional government of Germany from 1919 to 1933*). The Lutheran Free Churches and their leadership preferred a one party government, and therefore welcomed Hitler's move to ban all other political parties. Indeed, the Lutheran Free Church leaders looked to Hitler as the savior sent by God to rescue the nation in its hour of need.[57] From synod to synod, Free Church leaders were enthusiastic about Hitler and his gaining control of the government because they saw him as an agent of God's intervention into history. They also endorsed the old conservative Lutheran doctrine concerning the orders of Creation. This view held that in the sinful state of natural humanity, God, in his infinite wisdom, had provided orders of creation, divinely given structures of the human existence, to protect people against the consequences of sin and conflict. The state was one of these orders, along with marriage and gender. According to this logic, the Nazi state existed as an act of God in history, therefore, it must be obeyed as a divine instrument for the human community.[58]

It comes as no surprise that the Lutheran Free Churches and their leadership provided little, if any, opposition to the Nazis' obvious excesses and contradictions to basic Christian morality. They offered no opposition or comment about the persecution and deportation of Jews. When they did speak about the Jews it was a reflection of common anti-Semitic beliefs. Because of their support of the Nazis' regime and their ultra-conservative views, they posed no threat to the Third Reich, and, for all intents and purposes, were left alone. In the end, like the other Protestant churches, the Lutheran Free Churches never took a public stand against the persecution of the Jews and remained silent.[59]

Protestant churches were also silent during and after *Kristallnacht.* Following a parallel course with the Roman Catholic Church, most German Protestants merged their patriotism and nationalism to override any moral questions concerning the policies of the Third Reich. Many pastors eagerly went into the Army to get their names off the suspect lists. One scholar has written: "The failure of Church leaders to remain faithful to their own doctrines, to oppose the regime in obedience to the principles they taught congregations, meant in effect that they were supporting it..."[60] A revealing statistic that suggests the nature of the churches' silence during the Holocaust is that more Roman Catholic priests and Protestant clergy died in the German Army than were put into concentration camps.[61] Professor William S. Allen summed up the Church's response when he wrote, "And indeed, both churches gave abundant indication that they desired reconciliation with the Third Reich. They consistently showered gratuitous and unsolicited declarations of loyalty upon Hitler."[62]

Again, this is not meant to suggest that there were not untold numbers of individual Christians who in a variety of ways protested against Hitler's policies. Many ended up in concentration camps and large numbers died there. Some Christian leaders, such as Dietrich Bonhoeffer, understood that loyalty to Christ meant open opposition to the Third Reich. He and others were willing to carry their resistance to the point that they were involved in a plot to assassinate Hitler. The larger issue of a Christian protest against what was happening to the Jews did not occur and the Church remained silent. The events which included public humiliation and persecution of Jews, *Kristallnacht,* the operation of the death camps which engaged a large bureaucracy, and the transportation of thousands of Jews to "work camps," only illustrate how the churches remained silent even in regard to these public policies. It is obvious that loyalty and dedication to Hitler and the Third Reich took precedence over commitment to Jesus and his teachings. John Roth and Richard Rubenstein summed up the situation in these words: "Whether through failure to take Christian identity seriously, zealous commitment to a religion identified as Christian but fundamentally antithetical to Jesus' teachings, or some disposition in between, apostasy *(total defection from the Christian faith)* abounded in Christian civilization from 1933 to 1945."[63]

The churches have been singled out for their silence, but they were not alone. The professions in Germany were equally silent. The professions of education, law, science, medicine and government workers all seemed to align themselves with Hitler and the aims of the Third Reich. It is necessary to repeat again that not all members of these professions acceded to the Nazis because there were many who were persecuted, or forced to leave Germany, or ended up in concentration camps. The unfortunate conclusion must be that the Holocaust could not have been possible without the active cooperation and participation of all the professions.

It would be a gross mistake to assert that only the Christians in Germany were mute about the Holocaust. The rest of the world must accept its portion of the blame for silence about the extermination of European Jewry. Several excellent books have been written about the silence of the Allies during the Holocaust. The Allied governments were fed considerable amounts of information and data on the death camps. Roosevelt, Churchill, DeGaulle, and Stalin were aware of their existence and knew what was happening behind the barbed wire. Certainly the issuance of the Allied Declaration of December 17, 1942 denouncing the Germans for their "bestial crimes" toward the Jews, was evidence of Allied knowledge that something terrible was happening to the Jews. The location and names of four death camps: Chelmno, Treblinka, Sobibor, and Belzec were known to the Allies in the summer of 1942.[64] The Allied governments at this point were fully aware of the deportations to the death camps. Even with that information, the Allies were still reluctant to accept fleeing Jews into their countries.

The role and actions of the United States government in regards to Jewish refugees are a sad commentary on the anti-Semitism and indifference that forged our policies. At a time when Germany appeared willing to allow as many Jews as possible to immigrate, our policy, along with many other nations, was that of a closed door. During the Holocaust years, the Roosevelt administration would occasionally voice hope that the United States would once again fulfill its historic role as a refuge for the persecuted, the homeless, and the outcasts of the world. Such declarations were only temporary and carried no substance. The truth was that the Jews were not admitted, even under existing immigration quotas, throughout the war, no effort was made to change the quota law. While President Roosevelt expressed concern for Jewish refugees, he did little to help. Politically he would have had a difficult time changing the immigration quotas. Public attitude was opposed to allowing Jewish refugees into the United States. *The Fortune Poll* of April 1938, indicated that 67.4% were opposed to changes and in 1939, the same poll indicated that 83% were opposed to changes in the quotas.[65] Latent anti-Semitism in American society made its appearance once again, even after it was known that the Jews were being persecuted.

The infamous voyage of the ship St. Louis is an example of the indifference and anti-Semitism in the United States and other nations. The St. Louis sailed from Germany bound for Cuba on May 13, 1939 with 936 passengers on board, 930 were Jewish refugees. Each had scraped together $262 for passage plus an additional $81 as a guarantee for return fare in the event Cuba would not take them. The Jewish refugees were confident about landing in Cuba because they each had paid $150 for their tourist visa that had been signed by Benitez, Chief of the Cuban Immigration Department. But upon their arrival on May 26th, they found themselves caught in a web of Cuban political intrigue. On May 9th President Laredo Bru of Cuba had issued a decree that required refugees to carry visas approved by the Cuban State, Labor and Treasury Departments. Because of the political tug-of-war between President Bru and Benitez, the visas issued by Benitez were no longer valid, and they were not allowed to land.

The United States refused to intervene to help the refugees, and it failed even to consider the option of allowing the refugees to stay in the Panama Canal Zone on a temporary basis. This decision was made, despite the fact that of the 930 refugees, 743 had United States quota numbers and could legally enter the United States from within three months to three years after their arrival in Cuba or Panama.

After much futile bargaining, the St. Louis set sail for Germany on June 8, 1939. As they left Havana, a committee of refugees sent a telegram to President Roosevelt asking him to help them "of which more than 400 are women and children." There was never a reply.[66] In the succeeding days, the U.S. Ambassador to England, Joseph P. Kennedy arranged for the St. Louis to land at Antwerp, Belgium where the refugees would be divided up and sent to various countries that had agreed to take a limited number of them. They were sent to Belgium, England, Holland, and France. The story had a happy conclusion but only temporarily, because Hitler invaded Poland on September 1, 1939 and the war began. As it turned out, the only safe ones among the refugees of the St. Louis, were those who were sent to England. The refusal of the United States to allow those refugees to land is a page in our history that still brings us shame.

Churchill, of all the Allied leaders, was convinced of the horror that was transpiring in the death camps. The repeated requests by Jewish groups for the Allies to bomb the railroads leading to the camps, and even to bomb Auschwitz in 1944, were turned down for a variety of reasons. The primary reason was the overriding priority to destroy German military targets and oil supplies, even though Allied bombers frequently flew directly over Auschwitz on their missions. The second reason was that to carry out such raids would needlessly endanger the lives of pilots whose military missions were of more importance to the war effort. A third reason lies in the inability of many Allied commanders to believe such horror was taking place on such an enormous scale. Many termed the information on the death camps, gas chambers, and crematoriums, simply unbelievable.

The reluctance of the Allied governments to believe the magnitude of the Holocaust, despite the information that continued to come to them, obviously contributed to the death of millions of Jews and other victims. What is harder to understand is their inactivity, even after the whole picture of the Holocaust and its death camps became known. This is not to impugn the integrity of honest men making tough decisions in time of war, but there were, unfortunately, those in the Allied cause who shared the anti-Semitism of the Nazis. The United States government was as much to blame for the neglect of the Jews as any other government. Arthur D. Morse, in his definitive book *While Six Million Died*, documents our nation's indifference to the destruction of the Jews. Morse says, "As he (Adolf Hitler) moved systematically toward the total destruction of the Jews, the government and the people of the United States remained bystanders. Oblivious to the evidence which poured in from official and unofficial sources, Americans went about their business unmoved and unconcerned. Those who tried to awaken the nation were dismissed as alarmists, cranks, or Zionists…The bystanders to cruelty became bystanders to genocide."[67]

The silence of humankind is, in many ways, more devastating than the silence of God. The theology of an event will always produce mystery, unanswerable questions, and discussion about that which is unseen. Humans on the other hand, are very visible. How they think, speak, and act, is demonstrable to the observer or the participant in an event. Humans react and respond to their situation and their response is verifiable. It would seem, therefore, that the silence of humankind during the Holocaust is a great issue for humanity. The silence of other human beings, for those who suffered the Holocaust, must have seemed like another form of Hell. Elie Wiesel perhaps summed it up best, "Had the Jews in the camps known that Roosevelt and Churchill and DeGaulle and the Pope and everyone knew, and no one cared, I think they would have committed suicide."[68]

Discussion Questions for
The Silence of God

1. Explain why many people in the concentration camps came to the point of no longer believing God exists.

2. What is your response to Dr. Robert McAfee Brown's observation about whether the Messiah has come or not?

3. How do you respond to the idea that there is no such thing as "special providence"? Explain your answer.

4. Do you sense the feeling behind the questions asked by survivors and students of the Holocaust about God's silence? What is your feeling?

5. How do you respond to the silence of the German churches and most Christians in other countries regarding the Holocaust? What must we learn as Christians from this silence?

6. What is your response to the assertion that the real issue is not the silence of God, but the silence of God' people?

5

Facing Auschwitz

A pastoral letter from the bishops of the Danish Lutheran Church was read to all the congregations in Denmark, on October 3, 1943. The letter was written in response to the concerns of the clergy over the persecution of the Jews. The letter gave three reasons why the church must protest the persecution of Jewish citizens to the occupying government. The first reason was theological. Jesus, the Lord of the Church was himself a Jew, and he was to be the salvation for all humankind. The second reason was based on ethical concerns. The persecution of Jews violates one of the basic commands of the Christian gospel. Christians are commanded to love their neighbor, and no discrimination is allowed. (*Galatians 3:28*). The third and legal reason, was that the Jews are Danish citizens, and any persecution of them denies their civil rights and their right to religious freedom. The third reason concludes with this courageous statement: "Despite diverging religious views, we will fight for the same freedom for our Jewish brothers and sisters which we ourselves prize more than life."[69]

The Danish Church resistance to the persecution of the Jews provides an example of Christian courage and shows why the Church's commitment to justice cannot be compromised. During the persecution, Danish citizens helped over 7,000 Jews escape to Sweden. Only a little more than 500 Jews were captured and deported to the death camps.

When Christians are willing to accept the consequences of their faith and ready to put flesh and bone to their beliefs, the Church's witness is a power beyond itself. It staggers the imagination to think what might have happen if the Christians in Germany had taken a similar stand. It saddens the heart to think that when Christians in the Allied countries finally knew what was happening to the European Jews, they did not rise up in protest. Professor Robert Ross tells us in his study of the Nazi persecution of the Jews reported in the American Protestant press that, "The Jews are seen as a "deicide people," and only rarely does an American Protestant periodical dare to challenge this assumption…"[70]. Professor

Ross also reports that what most often appears in the various periodicals are the in-house issues of the church, not the higher Christian ideals of mercy, love, grace, forgiveness, justice, and concern for the sufferings of their fellow human beings.

We must learn from the Danish churches and from the theological implications of the Holocaust. Apart from being aware and educated about the causes and results of the Nazis' *final solution*, how should the churches prepare themselves? There have been many ideas and suggestions presented to address that question. Let me suggest that a beginning place for Christians is to re-examine some basic Christian beliefs if we ever hope to truthfully face Auschwitz.

One of the first Christian beliefs to be considered is the broader intent of baptism. The rite of baptism has lost much of its meaning within the Church. Although it is universally accepted as being the initiation rite into the Christian faith, the degree to which individuals are prepared for that initiation differs greatly within Christian denominations. For some, baptism is only a public declaration that the individual accepts Jesus Christ as their Lord and Savior. Others require a period of study and preparation before the candidate is to be baptized.

In either case, the commitment to follow Christ by taking a stand for justice, and mercy, with respect for the dignity of every human being is not emphasized, or is neglected altogether. There are some Christian groups who would go so far as to say those commitments have nothing to do with baptism.

Much of the anemia of baptism in many mainline churches can be traced to the practice of infant baptism. This is not to suggest that infant baptism is an invalid form of baptism, but the problem may be in the way it is practiced. In many churches that practice infant baptism, there is little if any instruction given to the parents, godparents, or sponsors, about the meaning and serious obligations relating to baptism. Too often, baptism of an infant is more a perfunctory ceremony associated with "christening" children, rather than engrafting them into Christ's body, the Church. Some wag has said that it is more difficult to obtain a driver's license than it is to join the Church. This is not to suggest that our practices of baptism are devoid of meaning or purpose. The critique is, that we as American Christians need to be reminded that Baptism is our public profession of faith and our commitment to be loyal to Christ and His Church under *all* circumstances. Loyalty, as Jesus said, must take precedent over family, friends, and must possess the willingness to sacrifice and suffer. (*Matthew 10:37-39*). Baptism in our time, unfortunately has become for many the gateway to cheap grace.

In our highly individualistic culture we have played down or ignored the meaning of community to our faith. It would be interesting to ask members of our congregations what it means to belong to a covenant community. Why is the covenant community so important in the eyes of God? If baptism is truly our engrafting into the body of Christ, where is that body to be found, if not in community? What do we oblige ourselves to do and be as a result of our baptism?

Our present day churches have become so entwined with money and membership statistics, that we have all but marginalized our covenant responsibility and lost our prophetic voice. The meaning of the gospel has become a quick fix for healing and peace of mind, rather than the call to stand for justice and mercy for our neighbor.[71] The reason for this state of affairs is that we believe in a *religious* God, in contrast to the Biblical God. Our understanding of the importance of the covenant depends on our understanding of God. The Biblical God can only be understood in and through the history of Israel. God first revealed himself to Abraham, and has come to us in our human knowledge through the history of the Hebrew people. God is not found in metaphysical theories, but in the "wholly otherness" of the people of Israel. As Professor Robert T. Osborn wrote: "God is as other from the world, as transcendent and holy, as are the Jews, the children of Israel, and as is the church the branch grafted onto Israel. Thus God's holiness, his very deity, is at stake in the destiny of his people."[72] The message is plain: God is known and understood by us only as the God of Israel, and it is only through the Jews that we know God.

The Biblical God reveals God's presence through the chosen people and God's promise of justice and mercy through God's partisan stance. The Biblical God is a fierce partisan for the poor, the oppressed, the downtrodden, and the helpless. God called Israel out to be the instrument of deliverance of humankind and to be a faithful community of justice and compassion. Religious acts of devotion and piety are not as important as are the acts of justice, mercy, and compassion. Just as the Biblical God, through the covenant, promises forgiveness, salvation, and justification for God's people, God also demands that the covenant people actively join in the battle for the establishment of a kingdom of justice and love.

This is the same God that Jesus believed in and understood. Thus, to separate Israel from our understanding of God is to deny God. One of the important lessons from Auschwitz is that to believe we are God's chosen people at the expense of the Jews is to commit heresy of serious proportions. Jews and Christians both follow and worship the Biblical God of Abraham, Isaac and Jacob; the God and Father of Jesus. It is the Biblical God with whom we have our covenant.

Conceptually, the religious God in contrast to the Biblical God, is not limited to or tied to Israel. The religious God, unlike the Biblical God, is not tied to history. Instead the religious God is above and beyond any group's history, and is to be understood only in a spiritual sense. Being outside and beyond history, the religious God can be experienced only in a spiritual way that transcends this world and material things. Professor Osborn says, "…the religious God is found, on the one hand, wholly "outside" or beyond history and the material realities of existence, and on the other hand wholly "within" the spiritual depths of the inner person."[73] Religion under the religious God allows the believer to 'capture' God to champion their cause. The God of religion can, in fact, become quite profane, by the willingness and proclivity to become the champion of any political party, policy, or program. The religious God can also be called into action for certain groups supposedly endorsing their particular position(s).

The danger, as Osborn has written, is that the religious God can be very partisan toward the political goals and ambitions of whatever political party is in power in a particular country. He cites how in 1933 the "German Christians" proclaimed that God was revealing himself to the German nation and its people. The God of religion was behind the call for Aryan purity and endorsed the leadership of Adolf Hitler as being messianic. The religious God can deter the Biblical God from interfering with or obstructing the goals, practices and programs of any group who claim God as their advocate.

The God of Abraham, Isaac and Jacob is the Biblical God. A Jew would not try to define God in metaphysical terms; rather, a Jew would seek to respond to God. The Biblical God makes demands, and if any representation of God is made that has no demands, it cannot be God. Normally, one who believes in the religious God finds few, if any, demands made upon them. Our culture's apparent infatuation with the religious God molds our strong commitment to individualism. Religious decisions find their ultimate authority within the individual. Because of the general acceptance of the supremacy of the individual to make all of life's decisions, the intrusive demands of the Biblical God are rejected in favor of the laissez-faire suggestions of the religious God.

If an individual, however, belongs to a covenant community that follows the Biblical God, the demands are more clearly understood and appreciated. Such an individual finds strength, support, and guidance from the community. It is from the experience in the covenant community that the individual finds direction and courage to follow God's demands and commandments. Telyveld states that the modern Jewish covenant community's understanding of the demands of the Biblical God is seen in a pro-active community light. "Most of us no longer observe the 613 commandments and cannot even pretend to be building God's Kingdom by faithful witness of personal discipline. For us, the demand of God challenges us to compassion and to respect for the divine image in every fellow man, much as *Mitzvah (the demand of God and the response of humankind)* eventuate in the *mitzvah* that is performance: *action in* the world in behalf of human rights, justice and peace."[74]

Only when we recognize our responsibility to act against injustice, evil, and the meanness of human beings can we affirm life and our faith. God is faithful to God's people and honors them when they respond.

If we are baptized into the covenant community that we Christians call the Body of Christ, we can expect that God will make demands upon us. Certainly, Jesus in his teachings taught that God expected certain responses from us. So the question must be asked, are we baptized into a religious God or are we baptized into the Biblical God? How we answer that question determines how we view baptism and its meaning, and our answer also determines whether we take being in a covenant community seriously or not.

This brings us to another pillar of Christian belief that must be examined. What role does the Holy Spirit play in the life of the Christian covenant community? When an individual accepts Jesus Christ as their Lord, and is baptized, they receive new life in the Holy Spirit. The Holy Spirit is the Spirit of God poured into the life of the covenant community. In effect, the presence of God is found in and among God's people. Through the centuries there has been much discussion over the activity of the Holy Spirit among the Christian covenant community. If Christians believe and accept the fact of the presence of the Holy Spirit within the Church, then it follows that God is present, and has some demands. What those demands are must be seen against *two* backdrops.

The first has to do with free will. If we can no longer accept special providence as a matter of faith, then we must look at the freedom of human beings to choose their course of action. Why humans are given complete freedom of their will is one of the great blessings and mysteries we associate with God. The covenant history of Israel reveals God's concern that his chosen people should fulfill his demands. Through the prophets, God's frustration is directed at his chosen people for their failure to remain obedient to the covenant. God did not and has not forsaken Israel. The Christian experience was that God provided the opportunity for Gentiles, through Jesus, to also be among the chosen people.

The presence of the Holy Spirit as promised by Jesus is tantamount to God's turning over to us the responsibility to fulfill divine justice, mercy, and compassion. The same demands God has for Israel, God has for Christians. The yoke of responsibility to be God's agents in the cause of mercy, justice, and compassion begins at our Baptism.

One of the messages coming forth from the theological examination of the Holocaust is that God is silent and inactive only to the extent God's people are silent and inactive. The Christian theologian Matthew Fox has written concerning this point: "It is human evidence that the God who promises justice and compassion is still alive, alive in his/her holy ones. In those who refuse to let us forget the evil that so readily captures human imagination and human works…God exists and God resists to the extent that humans do both in the name of God."[75] To be a Christian and to belong to a Christian community is our commitment to be and to act as God's agents, and to refuse or fail to act is to alienate ourselves from God. We find a deeper trust in God when we actively pursue justice, mercy, and compassion for others.

One Christian theologian, Dietrich Bonhoeffer, himself a victim of the Holocaust, discovered this truth while writing from prison. In his book *Letters and Papers from Prison,* he wrote: "Our relation to God is not a 'religious' relationship to the highest, most powerful, and best being imaginable…but in our relation to God is a new life in 'existence for others', through participation in the being of Jesus. The transcendental is not infinite and unattainable tasks, but the neighbor who is within reach in any given situation."[76] The true disciples of Jesus, from Bonhoeffer's perspective, are those who disdain the 'cheap grace' of the religious God and accept the 'costly grace' of the Biblical God.

When we respond to the need or the call of our neighbor, we are responding to the call of Jesus (*Matthew 25:31-46*). Our definition of neighbor is not limited to Christians, friends, or other moral criteria. There can be no authentic conversation about Jesus apart from the neighbor and likewise there is no neighbor in whom Jesus is not potentially present. Bonhoeffer put it this way: "…any attack even on the least of men is an attack on Christ, who took the form of man, and in His own Person restored the image of God in all that bears human form."[77]

The sins of the Church during the Holocaust amounted to apostasy. Priorities other than God's took over the Church's agenda. Institutional survival, rather than institutional sacrifice became the modus operandi. The German Church lost its understanding of what it means to be God's people, the Body of Christ, or the Household of God. They either did not have the discipline to remain faithful, or the courage, or both. Professor Franklin Littell summed it up: "The problem was, and in most of Christendom yet remains, that under pressure and temptation most of the church leaders and the masses of the baptized will allow their thought and action to be controlled by the demands of "patriotism" and the nation-state rather than hold the line even where the churches have drawn it."[78]

The second backdrop in our responding to God's demands, involves our understanding of belief or faith. In his book *With God In Hell*, Eliezer Berkovits makes a point about our misuse and misunderstanding of the term faith. "The concept of faith, as the term is used in the context of Western Christian civilization, does not exist within classical Judaism. One might define the meaning of faith in the Western sense as subjective affirmation of the truth of something, or the existence of someone, for which there is no objective proof. Nowhere in the Bible does such a concept occur, nor is such a faith anywhere demanded of the Jew."[79] Berkovits delineates the Hebrew word *emunah* that is usually translated as faith in our Bibles, but is more accurately understood as *trust*. Faith, he says, is not dependent upon the experience or the actual awareness of God. If these are present to a person, then there is no need for faith. He cites Martin Buber's categories of "I" and "Thou," and then says that our spiritual dilemmas are problems of confidence. Can we really "trust" our "Thou" in spite of everything? This he says, is not a leap of faith, but a continuation of life of the covenant. "The very essence of trust consists not in "leaping", but in standing firm."[80]

The difference between faith and trust is instructive for us, as we attempt to honestly face Auschwitz with all its darkness and doubt. The person of faith, says Berkovits, is forever with their "I," while a person of trust is always with their "Thou." We could say it another way; a person of faith is always with their religious God, while a person of trust is always confronting the Biblical God. When we confront the Biblical God, as we have already discussed, we are asked for our will. Neither acts of piety, nor pious prayers, nor burnt offerings are sufficient, only our will. Our response to the Biblical God, unlike that to the religious God, is intentional and not necessarily emotional. We, as God's people, do not wait to be called into service; we volunteer in every instance of need, suffering, or injustice. Indeed, our Baptism demands it.

Prayer is also a basic Christian belief that must be viewed from a different perspective. Today, most American Christians are practicing a concept of prayer that is born of special providence. Yet, when we put special providence beside Auschwitz and its victims, it proves to be non-existent. If special providence means God's direct intervention to save an individual or a group of people from sickness, harm, or suffering, then the Jews and Christians in Auschwitz bear mute testimony to its falsehood.

Certainly, the Jews who prayed desperately for the God of their ancestors to save them from the horrors of the death camps found their prayers to be fruitless.

Many felt that their prayers to God fell on deaf ears. As they continued to pray for deliverance, and conditions became worse, a quiet despair overcame them and as nothing happened, they could only think the unthinkable, God was either non-existent or had abandoned them.

One survivor commented, "I and others of the Saved Remnant are among the few of this world who understand what the death of God really means. We Jews of the Polish Jewish community lived with God as with an ever-available, always nearby Father who guided and sustained us and upheld our faltering steps. Suddenly, He was there no longer, we were utterly alone."[81] The fact that God did not intervene in the death camps, as millions of innocent men, women, and children were murdered, pushes us to surmise that either God chose not to intervene, or God has chosen to limit divine power in order to preserve the freedom of human creatures. By limiting God's power, God has elected to become powerless in the world.

To perceive that God is powerless in the world is very difficult for many Christians to accept. Most of us have been raised in an ethos of triumphal Christianity. We were taught that God is in direct control of the world and is guiding it into the future, when at an appropriate time (known only to God), Jesus will return and His kingdom will reign. At the center of such thinking is the idea that eventually, Christianity will take over the world. Evangelistic zeal to accomplish that interpretation of the Great Commission (Matthew 28:18-20) has given rise to militant Christian triumphalism. As a result, for centuries we have looked down upon all other expressions of religion and faith as being false, or at best, misguided. One of the lessons we learn when we face Auschwitz is that such militancy leads to arrogance and even violence against innocent men, women, and children. As Albert Frielander said, "Christianity can no longer live under the illusion that it is the Church militant, sword in hand, determining the future of the world. The sword has been broken, together with many illusions."[82]

Auschwitz has made us look once again at the Christ event. What many theologians have discovered anew is the meaning of God's powerlessness. It is by being powerless and weak in the world that God is able to be with us and in our suffering. Bonhoeffer spoke directly to this point: "God is teaching us that we must live as men who can get along very well without him. The God who is with us is the God who forsakes us (*Mark 15:34*). The God who makes us live in this world without using him as a working hypothesis is the God before whom we are ever standing…God is weak and powerless in the world, and that is exactly the way, the only way, in which he can be with us and help us."[83]

Bonhoeffer understood that through the Christ event, God had made it clear that he was not a God who intervened at propitious times and situations, and then retreated back to the heavenly throne. Indeed, as Bonhoeffer suggests, even Jesus at his most agonizing moment felt abandoned by God and was denied intervention *(Matthew 26:36-44; 27:45-46)*. In Jesus, God offers no simple answers to human suffering; instead God chooses to be in the midst of our suffering and pain. It was this insight that enabled Bonhoeffer to find strength during his own imprisonment.

The Roman Catholic theologian John Shea approaches this subject by suggesting that there are two views of God. One view is that of the "interventionist God" who is believed to be able to change the course of human history and events in individual lives. This understanding of God cures sickness, finds jobs, protects individuals from accidents, and helps teams win sporting events. To think God would help a quarterback win a football game, but would not intervene to save a child from being hurled alive into a burning pit, is to push goodness and compassion over the abyss and into moral chaos. The other view is that of an "intentionalist God" who, through the Jews and later also the Christians, has attempted to show that God's purpose in creation is to serve life and justice. God's values are revealed in both the Old and New Testaments. God intends for us to respond positively to God's commandments and values.

It is obvious that if we cling to the "interventionist" view of God, or even the "intentionalist" view, we will still be faced with the silence of God, or what appears to be abandonment by God. In this post-Holocaust period in which we are living, we are still commanded by God of the Old and New Testaments to continue to pray, whether we feel like it or not. Certainly from the experience of the Holocaust, some doubt that our prayers will be answered or even heard. If, however, our covenant communities leave the religious God and return to the Biblical God, the Holy Spirit will then be able to activate men and women to the "intentions" of God. In such an environment, prayers have at least the possibility of being heard. Perhaps as the Reverend Michael McGarry suggested, "One obeys (to pray), not out of simple duty or compulsive reaction, but simply because of the personally addressed command from the Creator God heard through the Jewish and Christian traditions."[84]

For many of the devout Jews who were in the death camps, the commands of God superseded their desperate situation. The silence of God or the sense of abandonment by God did not inhibit their prayers or responses to daily requirements of the Law. Professor Berkovits writes how, despite the pain and suffering surrounding them, many Jews found the strength to be autonomous persons.

The prototype of the autonomous Jew has been the story of Rabbi Akiva known from the Talmud. As the Romans were leading him off to his execution, it became time to recite the morning *Shema*. Through the centuries Jews recited the *Shema*, "Hear, O Israel : The Lord our God is one Lord;…" (Deuteronomy 6:4) when their lives were threatened or they were nearing death.

But Rabbi Akiva did not say the *Shema* because he was on his way to die. The reason he said the *Shema* was because, "…it was the time to recite the morning *Shema.*". Not because of the circumstances, but rather because he said the *Shema* at that hour everyday, as the Law required him to do. "To be unconcerned with what others may do to you, even when your life is at stake, because you are committed to the truth of your own life, is the supreme act of personal autonomy…. This kind of contemptuous indifference to the enemy is the ultimate of human autonomy…the ultimate of faith."[85]

Perhaps prayer, like the *Shema*, represents at its core a radical affirmation of a trust in God, despite where we are or what is going on, or when silence attempts to strangle our hearts. Prayer could be, as one survivor suggested, that God commanded us to pray as a gift or blessing to fill the void in our hearts when God appears absent and silent. Whatever position we take concerning prayer, it must always be subjected to the same plumb line articulated by Professor Greenberg. The warm and comfortable idea of special providence, nourished by our narcissistic individualism, when put beside the experience of Auschwitz is blasphemy. Prayer at its best is an act of raw trust.

The discussion of prayer introduces another basic Christian belief that must also be re-examined and redefined, and that is our understanding of God. As Christians, we cannot face Auschwitz with an understanding of a "domesticated" God. A God in the image of a religious God will not suffice. We must scan the scriptures, the history of the Church, and the Holocaust to see if we can find any substantial support for the God we carry in our hearts and minds. For most of us, whatever images and understandings are evoked will not, in all likelihood, survive the plumb line of the presence of burning children.

Some may feel such a plumb line is too harsh because it violates our comfort zone. We live in a time and place when commandments, duties, and obligations are regarded as intrusions into our personal space. Most of us are more at ease and at home with the prevailing cultural religion. Each person's religion is assumed to be private matter with a major emphasis to be a loyal and patriotic citizen. Cultural religion is the seedbed for the religious God. Hear the words of Field Marshall Herman Goering as he spoke at the Nuremberg trial: "I myself am not what you might call a churchgoer, but I have gone now and then, and have always considered I belong to the Church and have always had those functions over which the Church presides—marriage, christening, burial, etcetera—carried out in my house by the Church."[86] His is a great testimony to cultural religion and the religious God. Clearly such a view of God and the Church will not be concerned about the poor, the outcast, and the marginal in society. Indeed, such an understanding can assume God will not make any unreasonable demands upon the believer.

The Biblical God does make demands and does expect responses. Elie Wiesel wrote about those individual Jews in the concentration camps who took the Biblical God seriously: "There was a man who smuggled in a pair of tefillin, phylacteries[87].... He smuggled them in and there were at least two hundred Jews who got up every day one hour before everybody to stand in line and to perform *Mitzvah*. Absurd! Yes, it was absurd to put on the phylacteries. Do you know there were Jews who fasted on Yom Kippur! There were Jews who said prayers! There were Jews who sanctified the name of Israel, of their people, simply by remaining human."[88] From the expressions of Wiesel, Bonhoeffer, and others who experienced the death camps, the call to be intentional for God is more than a theological proposition. It is the difference between faith and apostasy.

Unless we are able to return to the Biblical God and away from the polytheism of the society in which we live, we will never be able to face Auschwitz. Until we are able to truly face Auschwitz, we are only preparing the soil for future Auschwitzes. As long as we follow a religious God, we will never understand the strength, courage, and trust that comes from responding to the Biblical God. Make no mistake about it, following and responding to the Biblical God requires a serious commitment. God does not want our spare time or our IRS charitable deductions. God wants us, our bodies, in God's service. If we decide to be a part of God's people, we *must* be willing to suffer for God in the world. Bonhoeffer spoke of the cost of discipleship with great clarity. "They (*Christians*) have an irresistible love for the downtrodden, the sick, the wretched, the wronged, the outcast and all who are tortured with anxiety. They go out and seek all who are enmeshed in the toils of sin and guilt.... They will be found consorting with publicans and sinners careless of the shame they incur thereby. In order that they may be merciful, they cast away the most precious treasure of human life, their personal dignity and honor. For the only honor and dignity they know is their Lord's own mercy, to which alone they owe their very lives."[89] These Gospel-charged words strike at us for our lack of trust in the Biblical God and our allegiance to the comfortable religious God.

The call to be a Christian demands a response for justice and mercy; just praying and looking on is not an acceptable posture for Christians. We learn from Bonhoeffer that Jesus is directly encountered when we open our hearts to those in need around us, regardless of who they are. He urged us to seek our experience with God through our ministering to others rather than through the piety of religion.

We must bring God down from somewhere "up there" and see God in our neighbor's heart. God demands that we seek justice. Our intention as disciples ought to be dedicated to justice. John Shea says: "It is the heart of God, the core of his being; and no one knows him who does not know justice.... The absoluteness and urgency of the claims of justice do not come from the solemnity of the law or from pronouncements from the sky. They are rooted in the earthiness of God. God is compassionate, suffering with, and taking into himself the pain and oppression of every son and daughter...Justice is the very life of God in man, his redemptive involvement in our pain."[90] This is a far cry from the domesticated religious God who makes no demands on us, and is ready to endorse our comfortable way of life.

One more thing must be said if we are truly to face Auschwitz. It has to do with our worship. Are we worshiping the religious God or the Biblical God? In Dr. Eugene H. Peterson's provocative article about modern day worship, he explains our dilemma of being open to change and reform, while still being true to tradition and heritage. Worship today is often laced with guitars, folk music, liturgical dance, light shows, rock music, videos, and hymns that remind us of camp songs and sermons on self-help.

Finding himself in this dilemma Peterson sought help by studying in the Old Testament accounts of the lengthy conflict of God's people with the advocates of Baal. When the Israelites occupied Canaan, they discovered that the Canaanite religion was Baalism. "The emphasis of Baalism was on psychophysical relatedness and subjective experience. The gulf between humans and God was leveled out of existence by means of participatory rites. The terrifying majesty of God, his *otherness*, was assimilated to the religious passions of the worshipper. The god of the bull image, and the god of wine, and the god of the fertility figurine were the gods of relevance, fulfilling personal needs with convincing immediacy.... The transcendence of the deity was overcome in the ecstasy of feeling."[91] Peterson says that worship in Baalism was reduced to the spiritual stature of the worshipper. Guiding the worship ethos of Baalism were the requirements that it had to be interesting, relevant, and exciting.

Yahwism (*the worship of the Hebrew God.*), on the other hand, was a form of worship that sought to make sure that it touched the intelligence and understanding of its participants. The focus of Yahwism was on the will. Peterson asserts: "The distinction between the worship of Baal and the worship of Yahweh is a distinction between approaching the will of the covenant God which could be understood and known and obeyed, and the blind life-force in nature which could only be felt, absorbed and imitated."[92] He also says that the biblical usage of the word "worship" suggests that worship is a response to God's word in the context of the covenant community of God's people. Worship was not understood to be subjective or private. "It is not what I feel when I am by myself. It is how I act toward God in responsible relation with God's people. Worship in the biblical sources and in liturgical history, is not something a person experiences, it is something he does, regardless of how he feels about it, or whether he feels anything about it at all."[93]

Today, in many of our churches we face what Peterson calls Neo-Baalism, worship that is designed to be an emotional experience, not a confrontation of the demands of the Biblical God. A person can be warmed, entertained or become excited in such a worship service, but probably not changed. The experience will be pleasurable and comforting, but the demands for doing justice and mercy, for looking for Jesus in the faces of the poor and outcasts will not be heard.

The religion of least resistance always worships the religious God or the likeness of Baal. Yahwism declares that there is something beyond the worshiper, and it is concerned with doing the will of God. We are no longer the people of God when we refuse to seek after God's intentions for us. If we are to face Auschwitz, we must give up our idols, our Baal worship, our religious God, and find the discipline and trust to worship Yahweh, the Biblical God.

It is painfully obvious that Facing Auschwitz is not a simple or ordinary task. To give up old and cherished ideas that have provided comfort for many years is an agonizing process. But when faced with the realities of Auschwitz, we have no choice, unless we wish to remain disciples of the religious God. When we do succeed at giving up our childish attitudes about God, we experience another level of faith previously hidden from us. That is what the Apostle Paul had in mind when he wrote to the Corinthians: "When I was a child, I thought like a child, I reasoned like a child; when I became an adult, I put an end to childish ways. For now we see in a mirror dimly, but then we will see face to face" (*I Cor.13: 11-12a*). Facing Auschwitz means putting away childish ways about God.[94]

Neither God nor Jesus will play the Lone Ranger role in our lives. God's presence will be where we find God's people and in the lives of those who are in need or who are suffering. We are called to be authentic human beings, the kind of persons that God has intended God's people to be. Jesus came to show us what the experience of being an authentic human being is all about. Authenticity is not determined by religious acts or pious words. Authenticity is determined by how we seek to be agents of justice, mercy, love, compassion, and service to those in need.

Bonhoeffer suggested that the time has come for us to give up religion as the authentication of our salvation, just as the early Christians had to give up circumcision as the authentication of their justification. Living out our lives, discarding all the baggage of religion and pious language, while seeking to do the will of God puts us in the middle of God's people and God's covenant. When we give up God, to quote Bonhoeffer, as "the working hypothesis," we find that the life of trust is exactly that. In living by the trust in the promises of God's Kingdom revealed to us in Scriptures and in Jesus, we develop a renewed sense of our discipleship. With a new sense of freedom, we dedicate our lives to seeking to do God's will, not just for ourselves, but for others, and in that process we find a strength and a peace that is deeper than we have ever known before.

Our religion does not define who we are; our integrity as individuals before God, and as a covenant community before God is our definition. Bonhoeffer said it best, "To be a Christian does not mean to be religious in a particular way, to cultivate some particular form of asceticism (as a sinner, a penitent or a saint), but to be a man (*an authentic human being*).[95] It is not some religious act which makes a Christian what he is, but participation in the sufferings of God in the life of the World.... The religious act is always something partial, faith is always something whole, an act involving life. Jesus did not call men to a new religion, but to life."[96]

Discussion Questions for Facing Auschwitz

1. What does Baptism mean to you? Where does commitment enter into Baptism? Should infants or children be baptized? Why? or Why not? What should be the requirements for Holy Baptism?

2. What is your response to the idea of a "religious God" as opposed to a "Biblical God" as Professor Osborn suggests? What is your response to the statement that "The Biblical God makes demands and if any representation of God is made that makes no demands, it cannot be God?"

3. Do you understand Rabbi Berkovits' distinction between faith and trust? Explain.

4. Do you believe God still intervenes in certain lives or situations? If so, how do you explain massacres, senseless killings, accidental deaths, and the Holocaust? How do your answers reflect the God of love taught by Jesus?

5. Do you understand Bonhoeffer's "powerlessness of God"? Explain.

6. Explain John Shea's distinction between an "interventionist God" and an "intentionalist God?"

7. How do you explain and believe or not believe in prayer?

8. What is your response to Dr. Peterson's comparison between Baal and Yahwism? Do you see the comparison in today's worship services in your church or other churches?

9. Do you think it possible for our American churches to really face Auschwitz? If "yes" how? If "no" why not?

Epilogue

"Then they also will answer, 'Lord, when was it that we saw you hungry or thirsty or a stranger or naked or sick or in prison, and did not take care of you?' Then he will answer them, 'Truly I tell you, just as you did not do it to one of the least of these, you did not do it to me."

—Matthew 25:44-45 (NRSV)

In Elie Wiesel's *The Town Beyond The Wall*, Michael, a young man who survived the concentration camp, makes his way behind the Iron Curtain after the war to his hometown in Hungary. The motivation for the trip is to confront "the face in the window." This face was the one that looked out the window on to the courtyard where the Jews had been rounded up for deportation. The face Michael saw in the window watched impassively and did nothing as the Jews were mistreated, abused, and eventually herded to the transport to take them to a death camp.

Michael finally finds and confronts the "face in the window." and when he does, he says to him: "'…Your duty was clear: you had to choose. To fight us or to help. In the first case I would have hated you; in the second, loved. You never left your window: I only have contempt for you.'"

"My voice was calm. It was important not to hate him. I concentrated my efforts to that end: to silence my hatred. Contempt was what he deserved. Hatred implied something of the human. The spectator has nothing of the human in him: he is a stone in the street, the cadaver of an animal, a pile of dead wood. He is there, he survives us, he is immobile. The spectator reduces himself to the level of an object. He is no longer he, you or I: he is 'it'."[97]

The thrust of Wiesel's thought is crystal clear in this scene; those who stood by and never spoke up or intervened when the Jews were being rounded up and sent to the death camps, were not worthy of being called humans. To be silent in the face of injustice, cruelty, and suffering is to deny our humanity and our faith. For

Christians who dare to listen to the sound of sheer silence at Auschwitz, this message will be burned into their souls.

As we face Auschwitz, we are compelled to ask the crucial questions of this post-Holocaust era. What must the Church do to recover its integrity and mission after Auschwitz? Can we still teach and preach an "interventionist" God after Auschwitz? Do we have the courage, spiritual or political, to address these questions? One thing that Auschwitz has taught the Christian churches is that a mute and passive church is no church at all. Further, Christians collectively or individually who remain passive in the face of social injustice or any action that denigrates the dignity of any human being are spectators on the way to becoming perpetrators.

Auschwitz is a wake up call for all churches to re-examine themselves to make sure they are not fostering apostasy for the sake of survival. Idolatry is the sin of preference in our culture. Money, material wealth, power, comfort, success, reputation, nationalism, and winning are among the most popular in our pantheon of gods. At any given moment, one of the gods of our pantheon can speak to us, and we are willing to follow, no matter the cost. The Biblical God that appears bereft of creature comfort rewards will, in most instances, be in second or third place. We as a society have developed a very sophisticated rationale for putting money, material wealth, and all the other gods of our pantheon in our primary place of commitment. Numerous studies conducted through the years have shown that we, as a culture, define ourselves on what we *have* instead of by what we *are*. The society and culture we live in appear to have more influence over our day-to-day decisions than do the intentions of the Biblical God. That is not to say we are a bad people; probably on balance, we are good people. Good people are usually defined as those who do not make any trouble, are patriotic, believe in God, and support their government. Most of the Germans in the 1930's were good people. This kind of goodness has the blessing of the religious God but not the Biblical God.

In this post-Holocaust era, it is appropriate that we keep the "in the presence of burning children" as our plumb line to measure our conduct as the Church. Auschwitz demands that we rethink our understanding and beliefs about God and what it means to be the people of God. Are we willing to understand that to be the people of God or the disciples of Jesus, we must, if the occasion should arise, protest the persecution, mistreatment, or any injustice done to any group of people in our society? And, if we know that any person or group is suffering from any unjust persecution, we must be willing, if necessary, to go to jail for the cause of justice. This is not a liberal social action idea of some ideological group; it is the demand of the Biblical God.

What would our world look like today had the German Christians opposed and resisted the Nazis' treatment of the Jews? Many believe there would not have been a Holocaust, as we know it. Daniel Goldhagen says in his book: "...the Nazis backed down when faced with serious widespread opposition. Had the Nazis been faced with a German populace who saw Jews as ordinary human beings, and German Jews as their brothers and sisters, then it is hard to imagine that the Nazis would have proceeded, or would have been able to proceed, with the extermination of the Jews.... A German population roused against the elimination and extermination of the Jews most likely would have stayed the regime's hand."[98] Protest and public action in the name of justice, mercy, or compassion is not, for Christians, a political statement; it is a Divine imperative.

Today's Churches have a massive re-education program before them. All Christians need to stand outside the barbed wire of Auschwitz to see what happens when apostasy is allowed to go unchecked. We need to look up and see the ashes and smoke billowing from the crematoriums and remember that because a lot of other "good people" chose to worship the gods of their pantheon and not follow the intentions of the Biblical God, these innocent people were reduced to ashes.

Knowing what we know now, if the Churches do not face Auschwitz with all its questions and doubts, it will be an act of blasphemy. Knowing what we know now and opting to be simply spectators in the presence of injustice and cruelty, will be an act of apostasy. Knowing what we know now, and being unwilling to protest, will be an act of inhumanity. The call to Christian discipleship after Auschwitz is the call to courage and sacrifice. We are called to resist evil, injustice, and cruelty wherever we encounter it.

Matthew Fox has said, "But resistance is also a miracle. It is the miracle of paying attention to moral outrage and responding to it. It is the miracle that connects all prophets and the prophetic spirit in all women and men. It is human evidence that the God who promises justice and compassion is still alive, alive in his/her holy ones. In those who refuse to let us forget the evil that so readily captures human imagination and human works. Existence and Resistance. These are the evidences of the Divine presence, however silent that presence sometimes appears to be. God is alive on earth only to the extent that God's works and creatures are alive. God exists and God resists to the extent that humans do both in the name of God."[99]

Suggested Reading

Bau, Joseph. *Dear God, Have You Ever Gone Hungry?* New York: Arcade Publishing, 1998.

Berkovits, Eliezer. *With God In Hell: Judaism in the Ghettos and Deathcamps.* New York: Sanhedrin Press, 1979.

Birenbaum, Halina. *Hope Is The Last To Die: A Coming of Age Under Nazi Terror.* Armonk: M.E. Sharpe, Inc. 1996.

Bonhoeffer, Dietrich. *Letters and Papers from Prison.* New York: Touchstone Books, Revised Edition 1997

_____. *The Cost Of Discipleship.* New York: The Macmillan Co. 1948

Borg, Marcus J. *The God We Never Knew.* San Francisco: HarperCollins Paperback Edition. 1998.

Browning, Christopher R. *Ordinary Men: Reserve Police Battalion 101 and the Final Solution in Poland.* New York: Harper Collins Publishers, Inc. 1992.

Cornwell, John. *Hitler's Pope: The Secret History of Pius XII.* New York: Viking. 1999.

Fiorenza, Elisabeth S. and David Tracy, eds. *The Holocaust As Interruption.* Edinburgh: T. & T. Clark, Ltd. 1984.

Friedlander, Albert H. *Out Of The Whirlwind: A Reader of Holocaust Literature.* New York: Schocken Books. 1976.

Gilbert, Martin. *Auschwitz And The Allies.* New York: Holt, Rinehart and Winston, Owl Book Edition. 1982.

_____. *The Holocaust: A History Of The Jews Of Europe During The Second World War.* New York: Henry Holt and Company, Owl Book Edition. 1987

Goldhagen, Daniel Jonah. *Hitler's Willing Executioners: Ordinary Germans and the Holocaust.* New York: Alfred A. Knopf. 1996.

Hilberg, Raul. *Perpetrators Victims Bystanders: The Jewish Catastrophe 1933-1945.* New York: HarperCollins Publishers, Inc. 1992.

Levi, Primo. *Survival in Auschwitz: The Nazi Assault on Humanity.* New York: The Macmillan Publishing Company, Collier Books. 1993.

Lifton, Robert Jay. *The Nazi Doctors: Medical Killing and the Psychology of Genocide.* New York: Basic Books, Inc. 1986.

Littell, Franklin. *The Crucifixion of the Jews: The Failure of Christians to Understand the Jewish Experience.* Macon. Georgia: Mercer University Press, The ROSE edition. 1986.

_____. and Herbert Locke, eds. *The German Church Struggle and the Holocaust.* San Francisco: Mellen Research University Press. 1990.

_____. Irene G. Shur and Claude R. Foster, Jr., eds. *The Holocaust In Answer...*West Chester, Pennsylvania: Sylvan Publishers, Ltd. 1988.

McGarry, Michael B. *Christology After Auschwitz.* New York: Paulist Press. 1977.

Morse, Arthur D. *While Six Million Died.* Woodstock, New York: The Overbrook Press. 1963

Roth, John K. and Michael Berenbaum, eds. *Holocaust: Religious and Philosophical Implications.* New York: Paragon House. 1989.

Rubenstein, Richard L. *After Auschwitz: History, Theology, and Contemporary Judaism.* Baltimore: John Hopkins University Press, Second Edition. 1992.

_____. and John K. Roth, eds. *Approaches To Auschwitz: The Holocaust and its Legacy.* Atlanta: John Knox Press. 1987.

Wiesel, Elie. *The Gates of the Forest.* New York: Schocken Books. 1962.

_____. *The Trial of God. (a Play).* New York: Schocken Books. 1995.

_____. *Night.* New York: Bantam Books. 1989.

_____, Lucy Dawidowicz, Dorothy Rabinowitz, and Robert McAfee Brown, lecturers. *Dimensions of The Holocaust.* Evanston, Illinois: Northwestern University Press, Second edition. 1990

Endnotes

1. Darrell J. Fasching, *Narrative Theology After Auschwitz.* (Minneapolis:Fortress Press, 1992). p. 4.

2. Elie Wiesel, "The Mystery and The Fear", Irving Abrahamson, (ed.) *Against Silence: The Voice and Vision of Elie Wiesel,* Vol. II (New York; Holocaust Press, 1985) p. 385.

3. Bernard Weinstein, "The Liberation of Ohrdruf: A Paradigm of Liberator Testimony", Franklin Littell, Alan Berger, and Hubert G. Locke, (eds.) *What Have We Learned? Telling The Story and Teaching the Holocaust.* (Lewiston/Queenstown/Lampeter: The Edwin Mellen Press, The Papers of the 20th Anniversary Scholars Conference at Vanderbilt University, Nashville, Tenn., 1990) pp. 196-197.

4. Christopher Browning has an insightful book on this subject: *Ordinary Men: Reserve Police Battalion 101 and The Final Solution.* (New York: Harper-Collins, Inc. 1992). Another book that treats this subject on a larger scale is found in: Daniel J. Goldhagen, *Hitler's Willing Executioners: Ordinary Germans and the Holocaust.* (New York: Alfred A. Knopf, 1996).

5. Elie Wiesel. *A Beggar In Jerusalem.* (New York: Random House, 1970). p. 200.

6. Robert Reeve Brenner. *The Faith and Doubt of Holocaust Survivors,* (New York: Free Press, 1980). p.93.

7. Johann-Baptist Metz, "Facing the Jews, Christian Theology After Auschwitz", Elisabeth Fiorenza and David Tracy (eds). *The Holocaust as Interruption.* (Edinburgh:Stichting-Concilium and T&T Clark, LTD. 1984). p28.

8. Susan Shapiro, "Hearing the Testimony of Radical Negation", *The Holocaust as Interruption.* p.4.

9. A.Roy Eckardt, "Christian Responses to the Endlosung", *Religion In Life,* 47, No. l,(Spring, 1978) p. 36

10. Raul Hillberg, *Perpetrators Victims Bystanders.* (New York: Harper Collins Publishers, 1992) p.264; see also John Cornwell, *Hitler's Pope: The Secret History of Pius XII.* (New York: Viking, Penguin Group, 1999) for a thorough discussion of Pius XII.

11. Hillberg, p. 265.

12. Cornwell, pp.296-297.

13. John Pawilikowski, "The Vatican And The Holocaust: Unresolved Issues". Henry F. Knight and Marcia Sachs Littell, (eds.) *The Uses And Abuses of Knowledge.* (Lamhorn, MD. : University Press of America,1997) p.411

14. Helen Fein *Accounting For Genocide*, (Chicago: University of Chicago Press, 1984), p.33. Fein's book is an in depth study of the Holocaust occupied nation by nation. Her comments on the role of churches in the genocide are of particular interest.

15. Fein, p. 94.

16. Irving Greenberg. "Judaism and Christianity After the Holocaust", *Journal of Ecumenical Studies.* 12, No.4 (Fall,1975) p. 525.

17. Elisabeth S. Fiorenza and David Tracy. "The Holocaust as Interruption and the Christian Return to History", Fiorenza and Tracy (eds.) *The Holocaust as Interruption.* (Edinburgh: Stichting Concilium and T.& T. Clark, LTD., 1984) p. 86.

18. John Pawlikowski, "The Holocaust and Contemporary Christology" in Fiorenza and Tracy, (eds.) *The Holocaust as Interruption.* pp.44-45.

19. Irving Greenberg, "Judaism and Christianity After the Holocaust", *Journal of Ecumenical Studies.* 12, No.4 (Fall 1975) p.524.

20. Greenberg, "Judaism and Christianity..." p. 529.

21. Littell, Franklin H. and Locke, Herbert G., ed. *The German Church Struggle and The Holocaust.* (Detroit:Wayne State University Press, 1974). p. 274

22. Des Pres, Terrence. *The Survivor: An Anatomy of Life in the Death Camps.* (New York: Oxford University Press, 1976) pp.50-70.

23. Levi, Primo. *Survival in Auschwitz: The Nazis Assault on Humanity.* (New York: Collier Books,1960) p.90.

24. Albert N. Fridlander, ed., *Out of the Whirlwind*. (New York: Schocken Books, 1986) p.167

25. Martin Gilbert, *The Holocaust* (New York: Henry Holt and Co., 1985) p.465

26. Gilbert, *The Holocaust* p. 434.

27. Selections could take place anytime or anywhere within the confines of the camp. See Robert Jay Lifton. *The Nazi Doctors* (New York: Basic Books, Inc., 1986) for a complete discussion of selections.

28. Andre L. Stein, "A Chronicle: The Necessity and Impossibility of 'Making Sense' at and of Auschwitz". *Jewish Social Studies* 45, Nos. 3,4, (Summer-Fall, l987). p.326.

29. Gilbert, *The Holocaust* p. 304.

30. Gilbert, p. 418.

31. Gilbert, p. 457.

32. Stein, "A Chronicle" p. 335.

33. Rubenstein and Roth.,*Approaches To Auschwitz* pp. 269-270

34. Elie Wiesel. *Night*. (New York: Bantam Books, 1982) p.73.

35. Reeve Robert Brenner. *The Faith and Doubt of Holocaust Survivors*. (New York: Free Press, 1980) p. 111

36. Brenner p.110

37. Simon Wiesenthal. *The Sunflower*. (New York: Shocken Books, 1976) pp. 14-15.

38. A.L. Echardt and A. Roy Echardt. *Long Night Journey into Day: A Revised Retrospective on the Holocaust*. (Detroit: Wayne State University Press, 1988) p. 72.

39. Johann-Baptist Metz. "Facing the Jews. Christian Theology after Auschwitz," E. Fiorenza and D. Tracy (eds.), *The Holocaust as Interruption*. (Stichting Concilium and T.&T. Clark, LTD. 1984) p.30.

40. Arthur J. Telyveld. *Atheism Is Dead: A Jewish Response to Radical Theology*. (Cleveland: World Publishing Co. 1968) p. 183. I am indebted to A.J.Telyveld for his insights.

41. Irving Greenberg,"Judaism and Christianity After the Holocaust", *Journal of Ecumenical Studies*. 12, No.4 (Fall 1975) p.529.

42. See Professor John Roth's discussion of Maybaum's ideas in, Rubenstein and Roth, *Approaches to Auschwitz to Auschwitz and Its Legacy*. (Atlanta: John Knox Press, 1987) pp. 303-308.

43. Richard Rubenstein. *After Auschwitz: Radical Theology and Contemporary Judaism*. (Indianapolis: Bobbs Merrill, 1966) p.151.

44. Rubenstein, *After Auschwitz* p. 153.

45. Emil L. Fackenheim. "Transcendence in Contemporary Culture: Philosophical Reflections and a Jewish Theology", Herber W. Richardson and Donald Cutler (eds.) *Transcendence*. (Boston: Beacon Press, 1969) p.150.

46. Rubenstein and Roth, *Approaches to Auschwitz*. p.321.

47. Jurgen Moltmann's views are fully explained in his book, *The Crucified God*. (New York: Harper & Row, 1974).

48. John Pawilikowski, "The Holocaust and Contemporary Christology". E. Fiorenza and D. Tracy (eds.) *The Holocaust as Interruption*. p.47.

49. John K. Roth. *A Consuming Fire*. (Atlanta: John Knox Press, 1970) p. 120.

50. Reeve R. Brenner. *The Faith and Doubt of Holocaust Survivors*. pp. 227-228.

51. Professor Aleksander Lasik reported his study to the *Annual Scholars Conference on the Holocaust and the Churches* held at Brigham Young University in Provo, Utah, March 5-8, 1995. He graciously provided the author with a copy of his paper.

52. John Cornwell, *Hitler's Pope: The Secret History of Pius XII,*. (New York: Viking Penguin, 1999) p.85.

53. Gordon C. Zahn, "Catholic Resistance? A Yes or A No", Franklin H. Littell and Hurbert G. Locke (eds.) *The German Church Struggle and the Holocaust*. (Detroit: Wayne State University Press, 1974) p. 232.

54. Zahn, p. 230

55. Zahn, p. 233.

56. John Conway, "God and the Germans: Political Witness Under Hitler", *The Christian_Century.*, Vol. 110, No. 17, May 19-26, 1993.

57. Kenneth Barnes, "The Lutheran Free Churches and the Third Reich", Henry F. Knight and Marcia Sachs Littell, (eds.), *The Uses and Abuses of Knowledge*. (Lamhorn, MD: University Press of America, The Proceedings of the 23rd Annual Scholars Conference on the Holocaust and the Churches. March 7-9, 1993, Tulsa, OK). Chapter 9. p.110.

58. Barnes, p. 111

59. Barnes, p. 114.

60. William S. Allen, "Objective and Subjective Inhabitants in the German Resistance to Hitler", Littell and Locke, (eds) *The German Church Struggle and the Holocaust*. p. 123.

61. Allen, p. 122.

62. Allen, p. 121.

63. Rubenstein and Roth, p. 201.

64. Martin Gilbert. *Auschwitz and The Allies*. (New York: Holt, Rinehart and Winston. 1982) p. 339.

65. Herbert Druks. *The Failure To Rescue*. (New York: Robert Speller & Sons, Publishers, Inc. 1977) pp. 1,6.

66. Arthur D. Morse. *While Six Million Died.*(Woodstock, N.Y. : The Overlook Press, 1963) p. 282.

67. Morse. p. 383.

68. Elie Wiesel, "Talking and Writing and Keeping Silent", Littell and Locke, (eds.) *The German Church Struggle and the Holocaust*. p. 271.

69. Franklin H. Littell, Irene G. Shur, Claude R. Foster, Jr. (eds.) *The Holocaust In Answer....* (West Chester, PA : Sylvan Pub. LTD.,1988) pp. 256-257.

70. Robert W. Ross. *So It Was True*. (Minneapolis, MN : University of Minnesota Press, 1980) p.xvi.

71. See Keith A.Russell's excellent book, *In Search of The Church* published by the Alban Institute, 1994, for discussion on how the early churches envisioned themselves.

72. I am indebted to Professor Osborn for the delineation between a Biblical God and a religious God. This discussion can be found in: "The Christian

Blasphemy", *Journal of The American Academy of Religion.* 53, No. 3, September 1985. p. 351.

73. Osborn p. 353.

74. Arthur J. Telyveld. *Atheism Is Dead.* (Cleveland: World Publishing Co., 1968). p. 170.

75. Elie Wiesel. *The Trial of God.* (New York:Schoken Books, 1995). p.175. Matthew Fox's comments appear in the "Afterword".

76. Littell, Franklin L., et al. *The Holocaust In Answer...*p. 347.

77. Bonhoeffer, D. *The Cost of Discipleship.* p. 195.

78. Franklin H. Littell, *The Crucifixion of the Jews.* (Macon, Ga.: Mercer University Press, 1986). p.76

79. Eliezer Berkovits. *With God In Hell* (New York: Sandhedrin Press, 1979) p.113.

80. Berkovits, p.124

81. Brenner, *The Faith and Doubt of Holocaust Survivors,* p.118.

82. Quoted by Robert E. Willis in "Christian Theology After Auschwitz", *Journal of Ecumenical Studies* 12, No.4, (Fall 1975) p.518.

83. Dietrich Bonhoeffer, *Letters and Papers From Prison.* (New York: The Macmillan Co., 1962) pp. 219-220.

84. Michael McGarry. "The Crisis of Prayer", *Contemporary Christian Responses To The Shoah.* Steven L. Jacobs, (ed.), (Lanham, Maryland: University Press of America, Inc. 1993) p. 137.

85. Berkovits, pp. 73-76.

86. Quote taken from, Franklin Littell and Herbert Locke, (eds.) *The German Church Struggle and the Holocaust.* (Detroit: Wayne State University Press, 1974) p. 24.

87. Two small square leather boxes with leather straps attached that contain parchment slips inscribed in Hebrew with the four Scriptural passages: Deuteronomy 6:4-9; 11:13-21 and Exodus 13:1-10 and 11-16. They are worn fasten in a prescribed manner one on the left arm and one on the forehead as reminders of their obligation to keep the Law.

88. *The German Church Struggle and the Holocaust.* p. 273.

89. Bonhoeffer, *Cost of Discipleship* pp. 124-125.

90. John Shea. *Stories of God.* (Chicago: The Thomas More Press, 1978) pp. 106-107.

91. Eugene H. Peterson. "Baalism and Yahwism Updated", *Theology Today*, Vol XXIX (29), #2, July 1972. pp. 138-143.

92. Peterson, p. 141.

93. Peterson, pp. 141-142.

94. See Marcus Borg, *The God We Never Knew.* (San Francisco: HarpersSan-Francisco, 1998), for an excellent discussion of this issue.

95. My italics.

96. Bonhoeffer, *Letters and Papers From Prison.* pp. 222-223.

97. Elie Wiesel. *The Town Beyond The Wall.* (New York: Schocken Books, 1982). p. 160.

98. Daniel Jonah Goldhagen. *Hitler's Willing Executioners: Ordinary Germans and The Holocaust.* (New York: Alfred Knopf, 1996) p. 418.

99. Matthew Fox's afterword in Elie Wiesel's, *The Trial of God.* (New York: Schocken Books, 1995) p. 175.

0-595-28145-1